Very truly yours
Russ Woodruff

A Backwoods Philosopher
From Arkansas

AN
AVALANCHE OF MIRTH

TRUTHFUL REMINISCENCES OF A PERE-
GRINATOR, WHOSE LIFE HAS BEEN
ONE OF CALAMITIES, HARD
LUCK, ACCIDENTS AND
FUN

———

BY

PRESS WOODRUFF
THE ARKANSAW HUMORIST

———

Over 100 Humorous Illustrations
By WALTER A. SINCLAIR
AND PHOTOGRAPHS TAKEN FROM LIFE

———

A FIREBIRD PRESS BOOK

PELICAN PUBLISHING COMPANY
Gretna 1998

Manufactured in the United States of America

Published by Pelican Publishing Company, Inc.
1000 Burmaster Street, Gretna, Louisiana 70053

Dedication.

To those who are sore on themselves and
everyone else, and to those who are
looking for a panacea, this sadness
remover and grief eraser is
respectfully dedicated.

INTRODUCTORY.

My Dear Woodruff:

If the Bundle of Sunshine for which you have asked me to write an introduction is the same jolly old package you have been tapping for so many years, then indeed will your readers be well repaid for the hours they spend with you. A Bundle of Sunshine? A barrel of smiles, hearty laughs, healthful humor and masterly character delineations—a barrel of wit that is clean, and of mirth that is innocent—a barrel of oil for the troubled waters of life—a barrel of healing balm for wounded souls—a barrel of cement for cracking hearts.

Peaceful be the passing of those Princes of Bohemia who, looking back upon the measure of their days can truthfully say: "I, even I, have brought happiness to my fellow man." More of human life has poured out through the floodgates of human tears than through the veins of those who have bled on glorious battle fields. Great warriors have made torrents of both blood and tears to flow, yet have we honored them. Shall we not honor him who dries our tears, who warms our hearts with happiness and illumines our skies with smiles—him who blots the great star, Wormwood, out of the firmament of our souls?

The sum total of hours of happiness that you have bestowed upon your fellow man, often without money and without price, should leave a large margin to your credit in the big ledger "way up yonder." And may the record of your faults be writ in water, is the prayer of your friend.   G. FRANK LYDSTON.

CONTENTS.

LIST OF ILLUSTRATIONS.

9

PRESS WOODRUFF'S ANCESTRAL TREE.

FIRST SPASM.

ANY ONE WISHING TO READ THIS MAY DO SO AT HIS OWN
RISK.

When I began writing this book I bought a gallon of ink, and a quart of pen points. I then pulled open the valve of my imagination and proceeded to record things which I believe will postpone old age.

At that time I had no worry or troubles; I was not then the victim of insomnia and chilblains. All the world seemed gay and mirthful as I perorated up to my brisket in the heyday of life. The hills about me were flooded with a crystal gleam and the woodpecker was soaring up to meet the rising sun. I do not know how often a woodpecker gets in the habit of soaring; that is his business, not mine.

I was happy then and the soft silvery radiance of hope poured in upon me like Heaven's own benediction. But now that is "called off" and I have taken on a heavy coat of gloom which is sticking to me like a mortgage to a North Dakota homestead.

The first thing I did was to noise the fact about that I was writing a book. I then went home and waited several weeks for publishers to come and purchase my manuscript. I was under the impression that they would fall over each other for a chance to tender their checks, when they learned that I was preparing something to quiet the nerves of a clamoring public. I suppose they were all too busy, or else they never heard the noise. At all events they never called.

The only encouragement I ever had to write a book came from a friend. He told me I should write one by all means, just to keep the running gears of my rhetoric in working order He also said that I should never allow the manuscript to get into print.

The only excuse I have to offer for placing this book within the reach of those who are looking for a good thing is that they can "catch" the jokes herein without resorting to vaccination. The book should be a specific for remorse and moroseness. It is intended to renovate a set of low spirits, and make them look like they are tailor-made.

I have made a desperate endeavor to tell the truth all through this book, but after carefully reading the manuscript before sending it to my publishers I find that by my own figures, I am one hundred and seventy-three years old.   P. W.

P. S.—Any one who has ever cultivated my acquaintance will be requested to pay double the list price for this book.   Press.

N. B.—A few of the illustrations herein were drawn by the author while the artist was on his vacation.

W.

TEMERITY.

SHORT time ago I was invited to deliver a humorous lecture in a Chicago jail. The people there are leading a quiet life, and the jailer agreed that a pleasing talk would help to break up the eternal monotony. It was on Sunday morning and the church bells were calling the faithful to worship. The prisoners were permitted to leave their cells and listen to a man with a story. I was surprised to find so large an audience. I lectured perhaps two hours and congratulated myself on the behavior of those present. No one left the jail while I was talking. After it was all over I asked the jailer how the prisoners liked my humor.

"Well," said he, "I did not hear many criticisms one way or the other; quite a number, however, requested me to take them back to their cells and lock them up until you had finished."

I thought perhaps my reading was too high for them; I had talked over their heads, as it were. Then I decided to go into the country where people know how to appreciate an evening of wit and humor. I started my advance agent through Indiana to bill me. He was accompanied by a trunk containing one-sheet posters, on which was printed the following modest announcement:

COMING!

——— THE ———

ARKANSAW HUMORIST

THE BANISHER OF SADNESS.

A Bundle of Sunshine! A Veritable Typhoon of Merriment! An Avalanche ot Mirth and A Package of Fun!

DON'T FAIL TO HEAR HIM!

The Silver Question will be Discussed at the Box Office.

Come Early and Avoid the Jam.

The Trouble will Begin at Three Inches past Eight.

Tickets---10, 20, 30.

When I started on the trip I did not feel that I was taking many chances. I knew that I could stay out until blackberry time and then pick my way home.

My first stand was in the town of Fowler, Indiana. When I reached that place I soon learned that my prospects for a large audience were slim, as the Glue Sisters were five days ahead and my advance agent four days behind me. Besides I had to play against Hood's Sarsaparilla and their paper was better than mine.

NO ONE LEFT THE JAIL WHILE I WAS TALKING.

The opera house manager said he did not look for a large house as there was a Methodist revival in town, the Odd Fellows were to give a grand ball and the Fowler brass band boys had sold 300 tickets for a concert that night.

I went to my hotel rather downhearted. I heard the

landlord ask his wife if she wanted to attend my lecture. She said she thought not, as she did not care to spend money foolishly.

While I sat in the hotel parlor resting my feet on the organ and wishing that I was rich, a little girl came in followed by a dog. She came up to me and asked if I would like to buy her dog. I told her I hadn't thought of making a purchase, but I asked the price.

"Ten cents," she said.

"What are you going to do with the ten cents, my little girl?"

"I want to go to the show," was her reply as she innocently chewed on her index finger.

"I am the show," I said. "I will give you a ticket, then you can keep your dog."

A thunder storm came up about 7 o'clock that evening and nearly all who came out to hear the lecture did not bother about buying tickets; they had passes.

To make matters worse, the four little "coons" I hired to distribute posters threw them all into a well and then went out to play.

When the curtain went up I noticed the little girl and her dog occupying front seats. They stayed until the show was over. They were about the only ones who did. When I had concluded I woke the little girl and told her that the show was over. As she walked out of the theater leading her dog I heard her say to herself:

"I'm awful glad I kept my dog."

My landlord had preceded me to the hotel. I found him still laughing when I arrived. I said to him:

"Landlord, what has tickled you so?"

"Well, sir, I tell you," he said, "I was just laughing about that last story you told. Gosh blamed if that wa'n't the funniest thing I ever heard in my life. Say, don't you know that boy of mine ought to be on the stage? Blame my buttons if he oughten. He's a natural born play actor. He just reminds me of you. He is the biggest fool I ever saw."

"GOSH BLAMED IF THAT WA'N'T THE FUNNIEST THING I EVER HEARD IN MY LIFE."

THE OLD HOME.

WANT to go back to the old home and fill up on green apples, then walk out into the blackberry patch and get covered with seed-ticks. I want to soak my being with recollections of boyhood days. I want to listen to the catbird warble an assortment of the sweetest strains of joy. I want to watch Mr. Wood Pecker as he flies across the field looking for a tree to beat his face against. I want a vacation from the mad rush in a congested city. I want to get away from the black clouds of coal smoke and breathe a breath from the fields of wheat and corn. I want to carve my name on a sycamore tree down by the old spring house. I want to grasp the hands of my kindred who knew me when a boy. I want to tread where my footprints have been rained out for many years. I want to go to the old meeting house and listen to a sermon preached from the soul.

I want to see the dogwood blossoms on the hill side. I want to go into the woods and watch the fox squirrel barking at his best. I want to hear again the thrush's song that reached my young heart. I want to look across the meadows and think of other days. I want to see the old swimming hole and count the passing years since there my heart was glad. I want to jump onto a brush-heap and scare out a rabbit, simply to let it know that I am still a boy. I want to hang around at night when all is still and listen to the whip-poor-will away down in the mulberry bottom. I want to hitch a mule to a bull-tongue plow and stir up the new ground. I want to sit down to a meal of corn bread, sow belly and lye hominy. I want to rest my feet on the jam rock and talk of war times, when the bushwhackers raised the very devil at Hickory Hill.

Some people claim that I was born in Missouri, while others say I was born in July. They are all wrong. I was born in Arkansaw. It was in one of those old time log houses which had a fireplace about seven feet wide and a mud and stick chimney. Some folks say that Arkansaw was made on Saturday night after all the rest of the universe had been finished.

After the war was over our folks were very poor. All pa had left was five children and a bad case of rheumatism in his left knee. Of course he had the farm of eighty acres, forty of which were under cultivation and the remainder under water. I can remember when I was teething the folks could not afford to buy me a rubber ring to help me along. The best they could do was to give me a stick of stove wood to chew on. When I grew a little older I had another teething spell which proved serious.

I was down with the fever and ague which hung on to me for eighteen months at one sitting. I had taken calomel until my voice rang like a tin pan. At that time an Arkansaw doctor never gave anything but calomel,

even if one had a broken bone.   One day as I lay in
my bed shaking the nine patches off the quilts with a
chill, I was seized with a fierce appetite for sour buttermilk.   It did not take me long to appease it.   In a short
time I was salivated and my teeth fell out like locust

THE BEST THEY COULD DO WAS TO GIVE ME A STICK OF STOVE
WOOD TO CHEW ON.

leaves after a heavy frost.   Every time I sneezed I lost
a fang.   Ma got frightened and called in the doctor.
He sat on my bed, adjusted his spectacles, cleared his
throat and proceeded to look wise.   Ma did not tell him

what caused my trouble, so his diagnosis was that my
teeth were molting.

The third time I teethed I hired a dentist to assist
me. He first drove a wire nail down to the second
section of the apex of one of my favorite molars. I

I WAS SEIZED WITH A FIERCE APPETITE FOR SOUR BUTTERMILK.

asked him what he was trying to do. He said he was
simply killing the nerve, a mere trifle. I begged his
pardon, as I thought he was trying to kill me. For
thirty days after he separated me from my pearls, I

walked around coughing up sections of alveolus. I think that was what he called it. For many days I refused to take any food except hot pumpkin and rolled oats. At last he surveyed my food mill and took my measure for new grinders. I can truthfully say that now I can read and write with my new set just as good as I did with my natural ones. If the new set aches at night I just lay them on the window sill and continue my sleep.

It is necessary that I avoid eating blackberries on account of the seeds; it saves me from leaving the dinner table and going out to the pump.

While we lived in Arkansaw, we children had to go barefooted. The bottom of my feet looked like hemlock tan sole leather. They were as tough as the feet of the girl in the story whose mother said to her:

"Sallie! look out there, you are standing on a coal of fire!"

Sallie looked around to her mother unconcerned and asked:

"Which foot, ma?"

When I was eleven years old pa made me a pair of shoes. He had only one last and it was for the right foot. These shoes kept me turning to the left all that winter. It did not matter where I started, I was sure to turn to the left and I have been left footed ever since.

Even to this day I have to be careful when I go out for a walk with a young lady. I have to take the near side. If I start to walk on her right I am sure to run into her.

Most of the farm houses in our neighborhood had puncheon floors. It was nothing unusual to see the boys and girls dance on them all night barefooted to the tunes of "Cotton Eye Joe," "Chicken in the Bread Tray," "Soap Suds Over the Fence" and "Black Eyed Susan."

The next morning it was easy to pick up a wash pan full of toe nails.

For a long time in Arkansaw there was no writing paper to be had. If a young man wanted to write to

THE THIRD TIME I TEETHED I HIRED A DENTIST TO ASSIST ME.

his sweetheart he would take a piece of pine board about a foot long and engrave the picture of an eye in the center of it and send it to his loved one.

The interpretation was easy. It meant: "I pine."

If she loved him she would go into the woods and get a pine knot and send that to him as her answer. That meant: "Pine not."

If she did not care for his love she would set the pine knot on fire. That meant: "I make light of your pining."

Pa had quite a nursery and he gave me a thorough training in the business. He taught me to bud and graft seedlings. Grafting requires a great deal of patience and practice to become an adept. Pa always allowed that at my age I could graft faster than any one he had ever seen. This was many years ago. I often stop now and think seriously how sorry he would be if he only knew what a grafter he made out of me.

Our neighbor's farm was an upright homestead. Kind of a hill side plantation. He always planted potatoes in rows up and down. This made the harvesting much easier, as he could cut off the lower end of the row, poke a pole or hoe handle up the hill to get the potatoes started, then hold a sack and catch them as they rolled out.

We remained on the farm until pa grew tired of chinch bugs and jimpson weeds. Then he sold out and started for the west where the children could grow up with the country. When we started we traveled seventy-five miles in a covered wagon to Baxter's Springs, Kansas, where we could get a train. At almost every farm house we passed on the road I noticed the chickens would get on their backs so as to have their feet tied. I have since learned that all Arkansaw chickens get into that habit from the fact that so many farmers move to Texas in the fall and return in the spring. The chickens always make the trip with their feet tied, and every time they see a covered wagon they get ready for Texas.

After several days hard driving we landed in Neosha, Missouri. Ma learned on arriving there that measles were epidemic in the town and like all women folks she thought we ought to camp and become exposed. She

BEFORE PA COULD GET ME ABOARD THE TRAIN I HAD TO BE BLINDFOLDED AND FORCED ON BACKWARDS.

believed that children should have that disease while young. We camped on the edge of town two days and got the measles.

In a few days we landed in Baxter's Springs. Every one was excited in getting ready for the long journey.

I was then fifteen years old, still barefooted and had never seen a railroad train up to that time. Pa bought me a pair of plough shoes, two sizes too large so they would last longer. I had on a pair of those tight jean pants which were about $1.50 too short. From the bottom of the pants to the top of the shoes I remember there was an intermission of about forty minutes. For a brand new Arkansaw emigrant I stood at the head of the class. Before pa could get me aboard the train I had to be blindfolded and forced on backwards. During that journey we children scattered the measles over two thousand miles of country.

A DREAM OF OTHER DAYS.

I WANTED TO SEE STRANGE FACES AND FOREVER GET AWAY FROM THE SONG
OF THE SCYTHE ON THE GRINDSTONE.

I ALWAYS HELP PA DO THE CHORES.

TO MAKE MATTERS WORSE, THE FOUR LITTLE 'COONS' I HIRED
TO DISTRIBUTE POSTERS THREW THEM ALL INTO A WELL
AND THEN WENT OUT TO PLAY.

WHEN WE STARTED WE TRAVELED SEVENTY-FIVE MILES IN A COVERED WAGON TO BAXTER'S SPRINGS, KANSAS.

TAKE GOOD CARE OF YOUR MA WHILE I AM GONE.

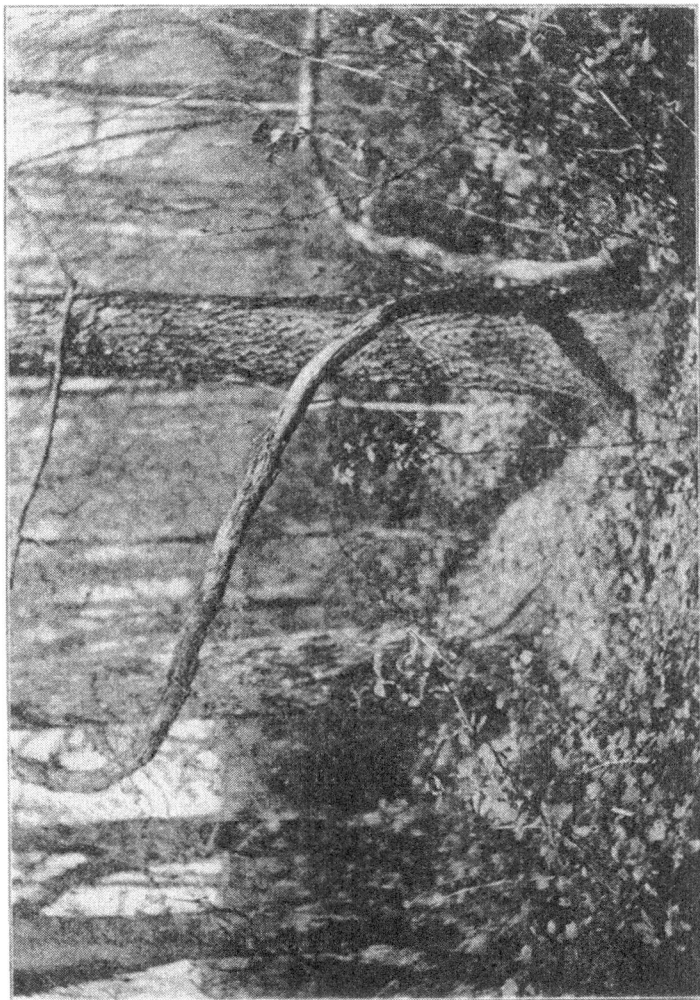

WHERE I MIGHT STROLL AROUND AND COMMUNE WITH WILD GRAPE VINES, COW SLIPS AND HE FERNS.

JUST A PICTURE OF AN APIARY IS ENOUGH.

CY. WILLARD.

EBENEZER EVERGREEN.

I HAD THE SIDE OF THE BARN AND ALL THE FENCES AROUND THE PLACE COVERED WITH CAPITAL LETTERS.

THE OLD HOME.

'TILDA GRIMES.

WILLIS AND JANE.

I WANT TO WATCH MR. WOOD PECKER AS HE FLIES ACROSS THE FIELD LOOK-
ING FOR A TREE TO BEAT HIS FACE AGAINST.

WHEN SHE'S GONE NO ONE CAN TAKE HER PLACE.

TRIFLING WITH MUSIC.

HERE is about as much music in a gourd fiddle as there is in a sapsucker sucking the sap out of a sycamore sapling. It was the only muscial instrument I had ever played upon or heard until I left Arkansaw. It has been said that my playing was the cause of our neighbors emigrating to Texas. My soul was full of music, and I longed for the time when I would get a chance to listen to something better than the high notes used in calling hogs, at which business I was past grand master of Elm flat.

In a town out in the state of Washington I went into a hotel parlor to hear a traveling Bachelor of Music rip off a few yards of joy on a piano. I must have looked out of place for I had just resigned my position as straw-bucker in a harvest field, but I did not care, I wanted to hear some music. Ye mythological gods and mountain trout how that man could play. He had studied technic, harmony and execution for twenty years.

With wheat straw and chaff yet in my hair, I had the nerve to address that noted musician. I asked him how long he thought it would take me to learn to manipulate the piano.

SHE HIT ME ON THE HEAD WITH THAT MAGIC WAND WITH MUCH FORCE.

"That depends," he said. "I do not know exactly, but I rather think you could learn in a short time. You look like a young man who might have natural musical talent."

I thanked him and went away feeling that I would soon be able to furnish myself with music enough to satisfy a hungry soul.

That very day I set out to find a teacher who would give me piano lessons. There was only one lesson giver in town. She was an old maid with a high temper and an ossified heart. She was the meanest woman I ever met. Even to this day, I would not talk to her over a telephone. The town folks said no one would live in the same hundred-acre lot with her, nor bathe in the same ocean. She had loved madly but not wisely. She had promised to wed a prestidigitator. He in a moment of hot flashes and forgetfulness had eloped with a chambermaid, and left the poor heart-broken teacher with nothing but a magic wand and her past to think over. She felt that she ought to get even on some one, and when I appeared she took her spite out on me. Somewhere in my peregrinations, someone had taught me how to play two chords, G natural and G minor. Now if you should ever want to try these two chords to see how they modulate, don't do it when you have company at your house if you don't want the people to leave.

Miss Alegretto, that was not her name, but that was the way she played and acted, started me in on my first lesson which was familiarizing myself with the treble clef. I have thought since it should be called the "trouble" clef. I worked awhile on that fleet of letters: f, a, c, e and e, g, b, d and f, and then I wandered off into playing my favorite G natural and G minor. When she heard that she came into the room with a rush and what a scorching I got.

She hit me on the head with that magic wand with much force.

"You can stick to your lesson, sir, or leave this house at once," she said.

"YOU CAN'T FOOL ME FOR A MOMENT.   THAT'S NO HEAD; THAT'S
A SQUASH; TAKE IT AWAY."

I looked foolish for a moment, then I got busy with that "trouble" clef.   Any time after that when I wanted her to do her little "turn," I could always bring her out with my favorite G natural and G minor.   She was always sure to make a hit—if she had her wand with her.

For every letter there is in music, there is a knot on my head, caused by the playful use of that magician's legacy.

A phrenologist came to town to give a lecture and I went to hear him. During his remarks he made a statement that he could tell blindfolded what a man was. A committee of three went up on the stage and tied a handkerchief over his eyes. It was then in order for anybody and everybody to go up and have their heads examined. Some one called out my name, and the committee came to where I was seated and took me up to the professor. He only felt of my head for an instant, then he said:

"You can't fool me for a moment, that's no head, that's a squash, take it away."

I did not stop to explain to him that the peculiar bumps on my head had been developed by the use of a magic wand.

After I had worked some weeks on the "trouble" clef and got a few more knots on my squash, Miss Alegretto started me to work on the bass clef. It was not until then that I found out that the notes on the bass clef were differently situated from those on the "trouble" clef. It was simply a different system. She was vexed more than usual at my ignorance and again got busy with her wand rehearsal. I took it all as good naturedly as I knew how, and told her if she would ease up a little and not get so handy with that magic club of hers that I would promise to marry her. That did settle it. I saw in an instant that I had made an egregious error. The last I remember was that I saw Mars, Venus, Uranus, Jupiter and many other heavenly bodies. It was about ten days before I could resume work in the harvest field.

THE WEEKLY PEAVINE.

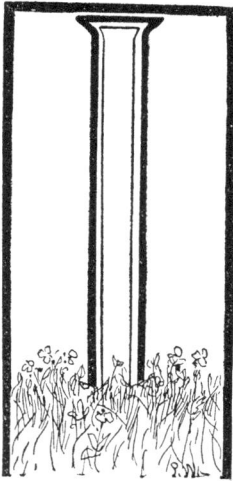

T is not generally known that at one time I published a newspaper. I have tried to keep this quiet, because the paper died young. It was devoted to the interest of the editor, and had the good will of all who got a personal mention. I had a guaranteed circulation of 200. This was necessary in order to get the one cent per pound newspaper rate from the postoffice authorities. The following clippings from the first issue give an idea of its tone:

EDITORIALS.

The object of the PEAVINE is to stand on its own platform and howl like a wild Digger Indian for any old cause that happens to be the style. We believe in belligerency on the slightest provocation. We are loyal, true and firm, and will fight to a finish on any proposition we advocate, as long as it pays. You are welcome any time at the PEAVINE office, where you can get the latest news and anything else laying around loose. If you don't want to subscribe for the darned old paper, it's all right. We will treat you to a cigar that will curl your hair.

We wish to state in this issue of the PEAVINE that on account of a drunken tramp printer whom we put to work some weeks ago, the PEAVINE will be something like twenty days late getting to press. For this mis-

IF YOU DON'T WANT TO SUBSCRIBE FOR THE DARNED OLD PAPER, IT'S ALL RIGHT.

fortune we are not to blame. We never were responsible for anything we could crawl out of.

* * *

There is a scurrilous report going the rounds that we have to go before a notary public every time we tell the truth. This is false. In the first place the truth never bothers us for a moment. We are as impervious to such reports as a slate roof is to a rain storm. Any man who has the gall to accuse us of tampering with the truth is a liar, a porch climber and an uncalled for excrescence.

*   *   *

We do not care to take sides on last Wednesday's shooting scrape. If Bill Rivers held a royal flush against a pair of deuces he should have taken the pot in place of a gun-podermic injection of bi-chloride of lead. It is our belief that Buck Watson has always been too handy with his gun anyway; and if some one don't cut his suspenders and let him go through the roof, we will not be surprised to notice a distance of forty inches between his feet and the bosom of this earth before another sunrise.

LOCALS AND PERSONALS.

Gus Henderson's youngest child swallowed an eggbeater Sunday night, and it caused quite a stir.

Bill Irwin has returned from a sojourn in Sedalia. He reports times very quiet. He says he did not miss any meals, but he postponed quite a few.

W. A. Roland dug a well on his new farm 1,200 feet deep and struck smoke. An injunction was served by the authorities and the work was stopped. Mr. Roland has since joined the church.

There will be a phrenologist's lecture given at Boggs' schoolhouse next Tuesday night. Heads examined and charts given in exchange for farm produce and dry cord wood. tf.

Don't forget the social hop at Joy's hall on the 4th. Tickets, including horse feed, $2.50. tf.

There was a new comer at Pete Tucker's house last night. Mother and child doing well and father happy.

Miss Eliza Rankin graduated on the organ at Peaceful Valley at the close of the district school. She will visit friends and relatives at Slabtown on the first.

Baldness is caused by the loss of hair. Use Potter's hair tonic, it never fails to leave the scalp free from dandruff—and hair.

Andy McLean took a drink of Spruce Gulch liquor while on his way home last Monday. The liquor was evidently bad, as he afterwards tried to pick the lock on his own trunk.

The new road from Pine Ridge has improved travel. Yesterday's stage brought in three gentlemen and one drummer.

Will Heartman fell over a fence rail last Saturday and broke his record.

Hereafter the Mount Comfort stage will change horses at the Ten Mile house. The off horse will be changed to the near side.

Lester Cornell took an overdose of "tarantula juice" yesterday. He afterwards collided with a freight train and got a caboose in his shoe.

Remember the Methodist festival Tuesday night. Already 700 cookies have been baked for the occasion. Admittance: Getting in, free. Getting out, $4 to $17.

Little Eddie Ross, after seeing the circus, went home and tried to walk his mother's clothes line. The funeral will be held tomorrow at 2:30 p. m.

A party of Coon Hollow boys seined the dam at Alter's mill last week. They caught fifty-two cat fish, one beaver and a set of old harness.

Subscribe for THE WEEKLY PEAVINE. Bring in stove wood, hay, spare ribs and molasses and pay your back subscriptions, as we have to live or die.   In either case, we are better off.

Try Joe Allen's new barber shop.   Shaving done without pain, or whiskers refunded.

WIT AND HUMOR.

Daughter (to her mother)—Ma! I wish you would make Willie stop.   Every time I hit him on the head with this ax, he cries.

Fond Mother (to her daughter)—You never use slang, do you, Sarah?

Sarah—Well, I should say nit.

Teacher—Now, Sam, what is a farm?

Sam—A farm is a body of land covered all over with a mortgage.

Teacher—Why did Lot's wife look back?

Sam—I don't know unless it was to ask Lot if her hat was on straight.

A WISE HORSE.

FEW years ago I went to Minneapolis, Minn., to make a study of the Norwegian language, as I had been informed the Norwegians were guilty of some very telling humor and got off jokes that often killed.

One morning I boarded a horse car for a ride. I stood on the platform with the driver so I could get the morning air, as that town is noted for air, both hot and cold.

While I was telling the driver the history of my past life, the off horse stumbled and fell. The car ran over him and the poor old fellow died in a few minutes. The driver, with an angry look, turned to me and said:

"You are to blame for that!"

"Why am I to blame?" I asked.

"Because you cracked one of those jokes of yours and the horse tumbled."

THE HEMORRHAGE HOUSE.

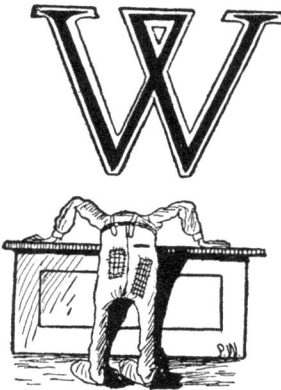

WHEN first I landed in Chicago all I had with me was a rubber valise and a striking resemblance to a farm hand. I could check the valise almost any place, but that pastoral look of mine could not be hidden for a minute. Leaving the Union depot I wandered down Canal street looking for a tavern. I noticed a sign which read:

"Hemorrhage House.
Strangers Taken in Here."

There was some comfort in that sign. I knew that if there ever was a stranger who had leaked into a big town it was myself. I reminded myself of a steer calf jumping a ten-rail fence, and leaving behind a green pasture just to follow off an empty hay wagon. I went into that pulmonary resort, that is, I suppose it was, as the name implies, and asked the clerk if he could give me a room.

"No, sir, I cannot, but I can rent you one," was his curt reply.

I did not say much, but I knew in a minute that he was an upstart. He was one of those flip, free, flossy, frisky, fresh, foxy, fluent festers one can easily discover in a city. He reminded me of the old story of the boy laid up with the scarlet fever, which had settled in his hair. It was as red as powdered cochineal. When he was a boy, he doubtless got too close to some speckled cow and she coughed bran in his face. He had a crop of freckles that would make a Missouri school marm relapse into a series of violent fits of envy.

I WANDERED DOWN CANAL STREET LOOKING FOR A TAVERN.

He asked me if I had summer fallowed that lower forty this season or sowed it in oats. I made no reply, as I knew he must be the village joker, and besides familiarity sometimes breeds distemper.

I registered my name, and the clerk rented me room
thirteen.   He said that room was the most noted one in
the hotel.   The first disaster he remembered was a year
or so after the hotel was built.   A robber got in through

'NOT LESS THAN 100 NIGHTMARES GOT IN THERE THAT NIGHT
TO GET THAT SACK OF OATS.

the door one night and choked a man to death for his
money.   A little later on, two couples were married in
that room.   Then it wasn't long until a man got up in
his sleep and walked to a window at the end of the hall,

jumped out, struck the pavement below and broke his neck. He said there were other happenings he did not like to relate. In due time I asked him to show me the room with the history as it was about my time to fly up and go to roost.

It was one of those small dark inside rooms with the windows down stairs or out in the laundry. There wasn't even a transom. It was just as dark in the day time as it was at night. I could never tell when to get up, and if I hadn't left a call, I might be there now.

The bedtick was filled with corn stalks and the pillow was a sack of oats. Not less than 100 nightmares got in there that night to get that sack of oats. Some were bay, some gray, several flea bitten and a few roan. They brought their colts with them, drank up all the water in the pitcher, ate up all the corn stalks and oats, then kicked in the footboard and left several sets of harness and horse collars lying around on the floor. The next morning when I went down stairs looking haggard and careworn, the clerk with garnet hair said to me:

"Well, old horse, how do you feel?"

"Oh, I feel my oats, thank you," I quickly retorted.

Then he grew angry because he thought I was trying to be funny, and he invited me to disband. He wanted me mustered out at once. I exhibited some delicacy about mustering and he assisted me. During the consternation I somehow went out the back way and had my right leg broken in two places, once below the knee, and once out back of the hotel.

After he cooled off I asked him why he called his tavern the Hemorrhage House.

"Because I always make my guests cough up," he replied.

TRIED TO BE A COOK.

I VOLUNTEERED to assist the Christian Endeavor Society in an entertainment to be held at the Presbyterian church at Spokane, Wash. One of the members told me that after the entertainment there would be a spread in the league room, and *all* the young men were expected to do the cooking. This was simply to add novelty to the affair.

I went home and asked my sister how to bake bread. She said:

"Why, in the oven, of course."

I told her to please refrain from trying to be funny, as that was my business and I could not stand much competition.

"Well," she said, "we women folks have quite a good deal of bad luck baking bread. We have to sit up sometimes until 12 or 1 o'clock at night to watch a batch of dough. To begin with you must set a sponge."

So I went to a drug store and bought a sponge. I got one for ninety cents, as I thought that would be large enough. For the life of me I could not imagine what a sponge had to do with baking bread. In the first place, I did not know where to set it, and what good it would do if I did set it, so I concluded to set it on the stove. Now

I have set bird traps, set up to see the old year out and the new year in, set up with sick folks, set up with folks who were not sick, set setting hens at setting time just to see them set, set up with other fellows' girls and a whole lot of setting up that I could tell about if the law

I CONCLUDED TO SET IT ON THE STOVE.

was not against me; but that is the first time I ever sat up with a sponge. The sponge had been setting on the stove about ten minutes, when my sister came into the kitchen like a cyclone.

"Goodness! gracious sakes alive! what on earth is that burning?" she asked. "It's just awful!"

"That is the sponge I have set for the Christian Endeavor," I said with a look of wisdom.

"Well! if that isn't the *worst!* Did you ever hear of such—gracious me! but if you—why haven't you a little bit of sense! The idea of setting a bath sponge on the stove, with the idea that it will turn to bread."

She then explained to me what she meant by setting a sponge. The next five hours she put in laughing at my ignorance, and she thought it such a good joke that she could not keep it. She visited all the neighbors near us and told them that I had turned out to be a cook. Anyway, I started in and tried my hand on flour, salt, yeast, milk and anything else that I thought would help to make dough. But to be up to date, when I got the batch ready I called it a sponge and set it. Then I sat up and looked at it until it soured. I did not know what to do in that case, so I called my sister and told her the sponge had soured on me. She told me to put in some soda to sweeten the dough. She did not say what kind, so I put in sal-soda. Then I kneaded the sponge with my hands and after that I needed liniment. But as sour as the dough was, I put it in the oven and baked it. When I took it out it weighed more than it did in the form of dough. I again called my sister to get her opinion of it. She laughed and said:

"I would pronounce that asbestos. You could not drive a tack in that bread. I would advise you not to take it to the church; if you do, don't let any one know you are my brother."

I was stubborn and set in my ways, however, and was determined to see a few of the members tackle it. I also baked four dozen cookies which I wanted to take along, but I could not get them out of the pan without a cold chisel. After a fruitless effort to remove them whole, I concluded the cookies and pan were good friends, as they seemed to be stuck on each other.

SHE TOLD ME TO PUT IN SOME SODA TO SWEETEN THE DOUGH.

With a heavy heart and a batch of sad bread, I found my way to the church in due time. I went into the league room where I noticed a long table loaded down with all kinds of bread. On each batch was a card, giving the name of the baker. I put my bread on the table and when no one was looking took the card from the finest loaf there and put it on mine. I put my card on the good loaf. I felt some better. I cleared up my throat, looked innocent and started around to shake hands and mix up with the people and act kind of sociable like, as though there had been nothing doing. Presently a robust young man sidled up to me and said he would like to speak to me a minute on the outside. I did not know what he wanted, neither did I know I had been discovered changing the cards on the bread. I went with him out back of the church. The net result was something like this: ! !! !!! ? * * * * ? ! ? * * * ? ? ! ! !

It was fully four weeks after that before I was able to leave the hospital.

THE RAZOR BACK HOG.

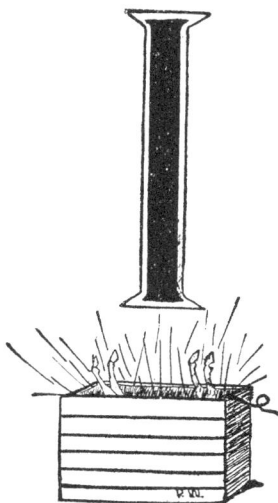

IN Arkansaw we do not raise the Early Rose, the Late Drum-Head, the Norman nor the Northern Spy hogs; but just plain, simple-minded, pickerel-faced razor backs. They can outrun a horse and drink out of a bottle with the ease and grace of a shitepoke. They have much hope of posterity, but no pride of ancestry. Every bevy of razor backs must have a leader. This leader is known as the bell sow. She is so called because she wears a bell that her where-abouts may be known at all times. She leads the other hogs usually where they are not wanted. They generally break into a farmer's cornfield and then trouble begins. He sets his dogs on them, but that does no good as they are too fleet footed.

From Turkey Trot, Arkansaw, to the Missouri line is forty-seven miles as the crow flies. A good swift bell-sow can make the round trip in seven hours and forty minutes. The razor back is the only brand of hogs to be seen at an Arkansaw fair. No Arkansaw farmer would have a hog that could not outrun a negro.

In the spring of 1872, Arkansaw almost had a hog famine. There was an unusual fall of rain, consequently a lot of mud.   The hogs that year got their tails so heavily balled up with clay that it tightened their hides so they could not close their eyes.   Consequently nearly every hog in the State died for want of sleep.

CONSEQUENTLY NEARLY EVERY HOG IN THE STATE DIED FOR THE WANT OF SLEEP.

The dry seasons in Arkansaw also work a hardship on the razor backs.   I have known it to be so dry there that the farmers were compelled to soak their hogs in water before they would hold swill.

SITTING UP WITH A CORPSE.

WHEN our folks lived in Roseburg, Oregon, I had more youth than experience. I was ambitious then and wanted to earn my first dollar. I was willing to turn my hand to anything that was honorable. The family was camping in a Methodist parsonage at the time. We were glad to be there, as it saved us making a bluff that we were able to pay rent. I remember the town folks were always kind to emigrants. One day a man came to the parsonage, and said to ma:

"I understand you have two boys?"

"Yes, sir," ma replied.

"Well, I would like to hire one of them to sit up with a corpse tonight. An old man has just passed away. The Odd Fellows will take care of the remains, as he has no relatives. Now, if you would like to have one of your boys come down and sit up we will pay him $2."

Before ma had time to say anything, I said: "I'll go, mister."

He said I must be there about dark and stay until 7 o'clock the next morning. The idea of me earning $2 in so short a time gave me hot flashes and made me dizzy for a moment.

53

The man showed me a vacant house wherein lay the corpse. This building was about three feet off the ground, stood on stilts in the center of a half-acre tract and was fully two blocks from any other house.

THE CORPSE WAS LAID OUT ON A COUPLE OF PINE BOARDS WHICH RESTED ON SAW HORSES.

Night came and I believe the darkest one I had ever seen. The corpse was laid out on a couple of pine boards which rested on saw horses. There was only one lamp and that gave a dim light. There were eight windows and no blinds. As I sat in one corner watching that corpse a rain storm came up and the wind howled and whistled as I had never heard it before. The night grew darker and the rain beat against the window panes like hail. The wind grew fiercer and actually seemed to say

I FELL ON MY KNEES AND REPEATED THE ONLY PRAYER I KNEW BY HEART.

something as it shrieked and moaned around that house.

By this time I wished that I was back in the parsonage. I knew that I could not stand that ghost-like drama very long, or there would be a new emigrant boy's face

flitting from branch to branch in another world. Just
as the storm was kicking down fences, tearing shingles
off the roof and beating its tail against the side of that
haunted house my pulse stopped. I heard the wild

I JUST WENT THROUGH THE WINDOW NEAREST TO ME AND
BROKE FOR THE PARSONAGE.

screams and harrowing wails of cats under the floor.
They yelled and howled like demons from the infernal
regions. It seemed to me that all the cats in Douglas
County had come together that night. They climbed
upon the window sills and tried to get in. Their eyes

looked to me like great balls of fire. I could not stand this awful suspense. I fell on my knees and repeated the only prayer I knew by heart. At the same time I kept one eye on the corpse and the other on the cats, trembling like a leaf as I listened to that fearful storm. I finally took the lamp and went into the adjoining room, a room which had been used as a kitchen. While in there the door blew open and put out the light. Then I was in the dark, and could hear the cats coming in at the door. The first thing I thought of, was to pray some more, but to save my soul I could not think of one word of that prayer. I did not have a match. I didn't even have a vest where I could feel for a match. I remembered as I went into the kitchen of seeing a shelf. I felt along it for a match and fortunately for me I found some. I lighted the lamp, got the cats out and then I went back into the room. The sheet had been partially dragged from the corpse and the face was turned to one side. My first impulse was that the old man had come to life and wanted to turn over. I did not stop to think that the wind had blown the sheet off. I put the lamp on the table and went away. I was in no rush about it. I just went through the window nearest to me and broke for the parsonage. When I landed against the door out of breath and with a bleeding face, ma was almost frightened to death. It took her an hour to pick the window glass out of my cheeks, chin and forehead. My nerves were so shattered that she had to sit up with me for two weeks.

YEARNED TO BE A MERCHANT.

BELIEVED from the time I was two years old that I was cut out for a merchant. As long as I had to stay on the farm, however, and put in my time cutting briars out of fence corners and pulling parsley for the hogs my chances were slim. One day I yoked up a pair of sway-back steers and hauled a load of wood to town, just to rest up and take a day off so to speak. It was impossible to sell wood or anything else for cash. It was a plain case of barter every time. I drove up to Jasper K. Jones' store in the town of Fayetteville, the county seat of Washington, which is on the road to Evening Shade. It is five miles from Post Oak Flat, in Allen township, state of Arkansaw. I asked Mr. Jones if he could use a load of wood.

"Oh, I don't know, my son. How much do you want for it?"

"Fifty cents in trade," I said.

"Well, I guess I'll take it; just drive around back of the store and unload."

After the wood had been corded up I went into the store and selected a fifty cent purse. I do not know why I picked out a purse, for I had no more use for one than a rooster has for a silk hat.

I thought it a good time to see about becoming a merchant, as Mr. Jones had plenty of time to talk that day. I braced myself up and went at him:

"How would you like to hire a boy, Mr. Jones?"

I ASKED MR. JONES IF HE COULD USE **A LOAD OF WOOD.**

"What kind of a boy?" he asked.
"My kind," I said.
"What is his age?"
"My age."
"What is his name?"

"Same name as mine."

"Oh, yes, I see, I understand exactly; you are the boy."

"Yes, sir."

"What is your idea of remuneration?"

"What's my which?"

"I say, what salary would you expect?"

"Well, for the first six months you need not pay me anything. I will be satisfied with just what I can pick up around the store."

He came to the conclusion somehow that he would not need a boy before spring.

PILL JUGGLERS.

HEN the Pharmaceutical Association held its annual convention at Green Bay, Wis., the mayor handed over the keys of the city and the band played "Welcome ye Sinners, Welcome."

The exercises were opened with a big entertainment at the opera house. The committee had me on the program for a short dissertation on incompatibles. The following is what I said in part. The reason I only gave it in part, was because I was never allowed to finish it:

"Fellow citizens and brother graduate lifters. I do not know why I have been called upon to address you on this occasion. I am not a druggist. Although I did serve an apprenticeship of three years, I did not learn much about the business. I was washing bottles most of the time. Speaking of incompatibles, I remember one afternoon while I was assiduously separating dirt from the bottles, a showman came to town with a stereopticon. He dropped into our store and ordered a bag of oxygen. My employer told me to make it and be in a rush about it, as the customer was in a hurry. I weighed out some black di-oxide of manganese and

chlorate of potash. I put it into a coffee mill in the back
room to grind it up. Just then I was called across the
street to witness a dog fight. There was another ap-

I WAS WASHING BOTTLES MOST OF THE TIME.

prentice in the store and I told him to turn the crank
while I was gone and I hurried to the scene.

"I do not know how many times that boy turned the
crank of that coffee mill; perhaps once, perhaps twice,
but I do know he went away without leaving his address.
He had no choice of routes when he left. He went

through the roof and took most of the shingles and raf-
ters with him. He had always been regarded as an
honest boy and had never been suspected of taking anything away from the store before. I can not say whether

HE WENT AWAY WITHOUT LEAVING HIS ADDRESS.

he found anything to hold to up there or not. Anyhow
he never came back.

"When I left that town two months later my employer was hauling lumber to rebuild his store." At
this juncture some one in the audience with a rusty voice

hollered out: "Rodents!" and the curtain fell. I thought for a while that the interruption was an accident, but I afterward learned that the scene shifter knew his business. The committee apologized and told me if I would write the menu that would conclude my part of the program. The next night at the banquet the following was served cold, and all members not in good standing were invited:

MENU.

Pickled Gamboge   Sliced Allium

Cream of Hydrargyri

BAKED

Baked Cuttle Fish, with Aqua Fortis Sauce
Saratoga Naphthalin

BOILED

Boiled Fresh Boneset, with Mezereum

ROAST

Roast Hen-Bane, with Benzoin Dumplings
Prime Ribs of Leptandrin, with Hydrastis Canadensis Sauce
Loin of Seneca Snake Root, with Vini Gallici Dressing.

ENTRÉES

Dimethyl-oxy-quinizine Pot Pie, Family Style
Minced Pepsin à la Credit
Poke Berries, with Sugar of Lead
Pan Roast of Colocynth, with Gum Tragacanth Stuffing
Citrine Ointment on Toast

SOFT STUFF.

Pilocarpine Sherbet

WIND-UPS

Shanghai Egg Plant Salad, Smothered in Carbon-Disulphide
New Frangula, in Cold Cream
Fresh Capsicum Pods   Mashed Cinchona

Belladonna Pudding

Digitalis Pie, Plain or Engraved

Iodoformized Cheese, Chloroformed and Emulsified for Summer Use

WINES AND WATERS

Antimonial Sec   Extra Dry Valerian Schlitz, Carbonized

Permanganate Fizz

Ice Water   Water Cress   "Water" You Think of Us?

Katzenjammer

R Zn S O4 grs xx   For a Chaser—Warm Mustard Water

BAREFOOT COURTSHIP.

T HAS long been a custom in Arkansaw to fall in love when quite young, then court for four or five years and sometimes longer. I do not know but that the plan is a good one. It gives a man a chance to find out whether or not his loved one toes in, and be sure that she tracks just right and does not interfere. A girl seldom has a chance to walk as she should in the summer time, as she often has a stone-bruise on one of her heels. In addition to this she frequently has a sore toe or two. You can imagine how she would appear in company walking around with both heels off the ground and a pillow slip around one of her toes.

One sign of love is when you see a boy's eyes shining around the door casing while the one whom he adores is passing. He is always backward, awkward, gawky and bashful. The first time he picks up the courage to speak to the one of his choice, he has enlargement of the feet. They seem to swell up on him like a pair of canvased hams. His hands appear to him like two washboards and what to do with them he never knows.

Two miles from our house lived an old residenter whose name was Silas Grimes. His only daughter was named Matilda, but they always called her 'Tilda for short. 'Tilda, to my mind, was the prettiest girl that ever made tracks in Turkey Trot township. Just one glance from her blue eyes was enough to give a boy throbbing of the heart. I had known her for several years before I could muster up the courage to side up to her. It was the fashion when a young man wanted to get acquainted with the girl whom he had selected to make miserable, to meet her at some gathering and take her home. That opportunity was usually found at the meeting house after the evening sermon. He would stand outside of the door and when she came out would slip up on the blind side of her and say:

"Can I tote you home?"

If she sacked him then he might just as well go to the house of some enemy and ask him to turn on the dogs, as he would never hear the last of it. I never cared to take such chances. I preconcerted a plan of action by which I could win 'Tilda's hand in a quiet way. Knowing that "a faint heart never won a fair lady," I thought the proper thing was to put on a bold front and go and see her. It was the custom when one went courting to go on Saturday evening and stay until Monday morning.

About sunset one Saturday evening I set out barefoot for the Grimes farm. The birds along the roadside were singing their songs as though they had a wildwood gathering all for me. A fox squirrel ran along the top rails of a worm fence fearing no harm from my hands. The sun sank behind the western slope and the night was given up to the music of crickets and frogs.

When I arrived at 'Tilda's house I stopped at the gate and gave the customary alarm: "Hello." Before I had time to think a pack of yellow dogs came from under the house all yelping at the same time. 'Tilda

WHEN I ARRIVED AT 'TILDA'S HOUSE I STOPPED AT THE GATE
AND GAVE THE CUSTOMARY ALARM.

came out of the house; grabbed a barrel stave and drove the dogs back under the floor before they had time to jump the fence and tree me. Then she invited me to come in. As I went in she blushed, and I blushed. I took a seat on one side of the fireplace, and she on the other. I couldn't think of a thing to talk about, neither could she. We just kept our seats and went right on

I COULDN'T THINK OF A THING TO TALK ABOUT, NEITHER
COULD SHE.

blushing. For a whole hour I sat there looking into the fireplace for salamanders and things and never once spoke. At last I got kind of brave and said:

"How is your ma?"

"Oh, she's just tolerable like, thank you. She's perter than she was and able to sit up and take spoon victuals. Her and pa went to prayer meeting tonight," she said.

It was not until then that I knew we were all alone and that I had the chance of my life to make love to 'Tilda. But what could I do? Every time I attempted to speak I blushed and could not think of anything anyway. Another hour of torture passed with unbroken silence. At last a mouse ran across the hearth and I said:

"I see you have mice at your house same as we have."

"Yes, sir," was her only reply.

Then another duration of painful silence set in. At last she told me the room for company was upstairs and I could go there any time I liked. The upstairs was the loft, and the stairway was a ladder leading through a hole three feet square. I bid 'Tilda good night and took to the ladder. I was glad to be alone once more. I crawled into the straw bed and thought it all over. I would have signed a contract to put in Grimes' entire crop free of charge if I could have been home.

The next morning I heard Mr. Grimes call 'Tilda. He told her it was time to get up and cook breakfast. I also heard him joking her about her new beau. Then I could feel my face turn red. I made up my mind to get out of that house some way and go home. I did not want to stay for breakfast. There was no window through which I could make my escape, but I soon discovered a stove hole. I dressed myself and tried to get through that hole, but I could only go part way and had to crawfish. An idea dawned upon me that if I should remove my trousers it would reduce my size, then perhaps I could get through. This time I managed to get through as far as my waist, but could go no farther, neither could I get back. I was stuck as fast

as a wooden glut in an elm log. It was an awful pre-
dicament, and to make matters worse, a calf had found
my trousers, which I had thrown to the ground, and was
chewing them up.

ALL I COULD DO WAS WIGGLE AND WATCH THAT CALF GET
BUSY WITH MY PANTS.

Just then I heard Mr. Grimes calling me to breakfast, but I could not answer him as the talking part of
me was on the outside of the house. All I could do
was to wiggle and watch that calf get busy with my

pants. It wasn't long until Mr. Grimes called me again, but there was no answer. I heard him climbing the ladder; he wanted to know, of course, the cause of my silence. He said:

"Good morning."

I also said: "Good morning," but no one heard me but the calf and it was too busy to look up. Mr. Grimes got a crowbar and pried the logs apart so I could get back into the room. Then he hollered down the ladder:

"Ma, you an' 'Tilda git out'n the sittin' room, 'case the new beau is comin' down, an' he ain't comin' head fust nuther."

When I got out of that house I saw that the calf had about finished my pants and there was no use of me hanging around there. So I jumped the fence and broke for home pantless.

In order to avoid meeting any one I took a new cut road and as luck would have it I met a number of boys and girls returning from a dance over at Gilbert's schoolhouse. I passed by them so fast, however, that they did not know whether I was a boy or a dog.

Two years elapsed during which time I never laid eyes on 'Tilda, yet I loved her.

One day pa sent Bill and I to clear some land not far from the Grimes place. I looked down the road and I saw 'Tilda coming. In some way I wanted to let her know that I still thought well of her. Close to the road was a hickory tree upon which I was chopping. I thought to myself that when she came up even with the tree I would show off some, and let her see what an adept I was with an ax. I had the air full of chips as she approached. Just then one of those rusty lizards took refuge up my pants' leg. I forgot all about 'Tilda in my mad rush to remove my jeans. This did no good, however, as the lizard was rapidly journeying up my back, and before I knew what I was doing I had also shucked my shirt in my effort to get rid of that blue bellied pest.

THE LIZZARD WAS RAPIDLY JOURNEYING UP MY BACK.

When I came to my senses I looked around for 'Tilda. She was not to be seen, but down the road a mile or so was a big cloud of dust.

After that I persuaded pa to sell out and emigrate to Oregon.

A CEDAR OF LEBANON.

URING the winter of 1895 I slipped into the state of Minnesota unobserved. I had written a new lecture and I wanted to try it on strangers. The old saying, that a prophet in his own country is a dead one, is correct. I have tried it and know whereof I speak. Bloody treason did not flourish over me, but other things did.

In the city of Brainerd I was employed by the Ancient Order of United Workmen to give an evening of mirth. I had to wait several days as the show was to be given far into the middle of the month. I put up at the "Rest for the Weary" hotel. On account of the Bacchanalian buffet next door, there were plenty of weary men who certainly needed rest. The brand of squirrel whiskey they sold would kill, embalm, dry up the insides, mummify and tan the hides of mice, bugs, birds, rats, dogs and men.

The night before the show I passed through that bureau of convenience. Standing at the bar I noticed an old man bent with age and bent on getting full of booze. His much out of place soliloquy caused me to inquire who and what he was. He lived up in the woods some sixty miles from that place and about twice a year he came to town for the purpose of collecting a well regulated, hand painted symmetrical jag. When he had collected about so much he would forget his whereabouts and talk Scripture to himself. While he leaned over the bar I heard him say:

"I am one of the (hic) cedars of Lebanon, and (hic) Moses was a friend of mine."

I went on into the hotel office, picked up a daily paper and took a chair near the stove. The old fellow came in shortly afterward, followed by his dog. He dropped into a chair near me with his faithful canine by his side. He crossed his legs, closed his eyes and expectorated in any direction his face happened to be turned. As he sat there with wild, feverish, muddled thoughts chasing each other through his bewildered brain, this is what he said:

"I am one of the cedars of Lebanon, and I tell (hic) you right here, that Pharaoh was no friend of mine. He was a plutocrat, and (hic) Moses gave him the worst end of it. Moses was a square (hic) kind of a fellow and Pharaoh tried to do him dirt. Moses told (hic) Pharaoh that if he didn't liberate the children of Israel he would rain frogs in the land of Egypt nine feet deep. Pharaoh gave him the horse laugh (hic) and told him that nary children would he let free, and he could start in and do his dirty work as soon as he liked. Moses (hic) took a turn around the block and thought it all over. (Lie down, Tige, lie down (hic); don't be such a bad dog, I'll (hic) take you home tomorrow). He fully decided to rain the frogs just to show Pharaoh that he was as (hic) good as his word. Well, say! you ought to have seen that shower (hic) of frogs coming down. There was bull frogs, big frogs, slim ones,

fat ones (hic), green frogs and frogs.   Pharaoh had
frog horrors.   They were sticking to him like glue.

"Pharaoh got (hic) sick of the greenback visitors
and sent Moses a message asking him to report at his

"I AM ONE OF THE CEDARS OF LEBANON."

office as soon as possible, as he wanted (hic) to see
him on some important business.   Moses laughed in his
sleeve when (hic) he read the message and said he
guessed he had Pharaoh on the run.   When Moses
showed up at Pharaoh's office, Pharaoh (hic) told him

if he would clean up the frogs he could (hic) go over to the land of Goshen, take the children of Israel and get clean to the devil (hic) out of the country. (Lie down, Tige (hic); lie down, you snoozer, and behave.) Moses ordered his carriage and drove (hic) over to Goshen. He gave orders to the children to pack up their trunks and get ready (hic) for a forty years' vacation in the wilderness.

"In the meantime (hic) Pharaoh had experienced a hardening of the heart and he telephoned (hic) Moses to please report at his office again. Moses couldn't think what the old man had been smoking, but (hic) he complied with his request anyway. Pharaoh told him that he had changed his mind. He would not free the children from bondage, as he thought (hic) they ought to remain under his protection. Then (hic) Moses got his dander up and called Pharaoh an old fossil and a degenerate, and (hic) furthermore told him if he did not free the children, he would rain lice and darkness (hic) all over Egypt.

"Pharaoh laughed at his threats and told him to (hic) go right ahead and get busy. I guess he was the busiest man in all of Egypt for a while (hic) the way he rained lice and darkness. Say! you ought to have been there! Egypt was the lousiest country on earth. Moses kept Pharaoh guessing more than the city election. He hoisted a white flag and cried for light and a lice clean up. Yes, he told Moses to take away the plague and then he could (hic) take the children, skip out, and stay out. So Moses (lie down, Tige, don't be so nervous, I'll feed you soon!) boarded a horse (hic) car and went back to Goshen. He told the children to get a move on themselves, as they had to start out that night. He gave (hic) orders to make great haste, as the man with the ossified heart might back out before they could get away. They (hic) were all well on the road to the Red Sea, when Pharaoh had another bad attack of hardened heart. He swore he would overtake Moses and the children and

HE SWORE HE WOULD OVERTAKE MOSES.

bring them back. So he called out the State Militia, a lot of express wagons, chariots, and the entire police force and away he went down the county road (hic) after the children, dead bent on overtaking them. Of course Moses and the children had a cinch. They passed across the Red Sea on dry land and reached the other side safely. Pharaoh was chump enough to think he could do the same (hic) thing, but when he and his army of "lobsters" got about half way across, they all at once inhaled too much of the water and that settled them. But that is neither here (hic) nor there, that's all over with now, but for all that I am one (hic) of the cedars of Lebanon.

"Say! Don't you know that I have been married three times? My first wife (hic) was a terror, that's what she was. I got sick of her one day and left, or she left me (hic)—I don't remember which. My second wife had a crazy notion that she (hic) wanted all the furniture in town. She (hic) kept talking furniture and I kept buying until I had the back yard full of it. One day (hic) I got so angry at her that I broke for the tall pines. I built me a hut (hic) and lived there for eight years in peace. One day I went to a little town (hic) and there I met a woman who was a peach. Say, but she was a dream (lie down, Tige, we'll go soon!). She had on gorgeous vestments and other things. I fell in love with her, and to make (hic) a long story short, I married her. And by gosh, we hadn't been married twenty-four hours before I found out that she had been my second wife eight years previous. (Lie down, Tige, we'll go home soon, old fellow)."

Then the old man passed into a sleep that looked good for fifty years.

HOMESICK.

AST night I fell asleep and began to dream. I saw a horse leave his oats and come to me. He was a poor old meek-eyed, sway-back, sore-footed car horse. With a sad face he begged leave to tell me his troubles. I told him to go ahead and if his troubles were more than mine I would treat him to a bale of hay.

"Speak ye not jestingly, kind sir, for I am almost blind," he said. "I am poor and weak. My suffering is much and my tortures are many. See ye not my many infirmities? I am stricken with sweeney and bone spavin. Look at that pole-evil on my neck. My ankles are stocked from standing in bad stalls. See ye the length of my fetlocks; they have not been trimmed for many months. Look ye, oh sir, with tears in your eyes and a sad heart at the string halt with which I am afflicted. I am a victim of the heaves, caused by eating dusty hay through the neglect of my hostler. He never wets my feed nor does he pick the briars out of my hay. For many years—I say years because our years are months— I have been in the carette service running from the Union depot to North avenue, in Chicago. I have had hundreds of hard falls on the cobble stones from wearing slick shoes. I am weary of life and my days are numbered. Through the cold blasts of winter and the sweltering heat of summer I have drawn these carettes without complaining and now——"

"MY SUFFERING IS MUCH AND MY TORTURES ARE MANY."

"Excuse me, old horse, for interrupting you, but I will go this minute and see the officers of the Humane society; they will take up your case at once."

As I started toward the city hall the horse grabbed me by the coat with his teeth and lifted me off the ground.

"I entreat thee to listen to my pleading. Be thou not in great haste, for in it the speed is slow. Know ye not that the Humane society is no longer worthy of that name? Better far it be called the Hot Air League. Thou can see with thine own eyes that I am reduced to a stack of bones waiting for that Humane society to come and rescue the perishing. Turn thou not away, but rather bestow upon me a great blessing. Gather together a few shekels, buy me from my owner and lead me to my home in Indiana. There turn me loose in the green fields of high grass where the running brooks are many. I know I am only a horse but I have feeling. Would thou seek to take my place and draw that carette for a single day and allow the driver to beat the hair off thee? I have many times prayed that I might be a mule. Then I would kick in the dashboard of that carette. I would fear no prosecution for being the direct cause of the driver's funeral. But that is not my disposition. I have always been kind, gentle and easy to curry from my colthood. I implore thee, good sir, to grant me the favor I have asked. Lead me to my home that I may escape the awful stigma which will be inflicted upon me. It is my last request, please take me away, sir, for the thoughts of dropping dead on the streets of Chicago will certainly drive me mad."

I awoke with a start, sat up erect and looked wildly about me; and then—I swore I would take the deviled ham and mince pie cure before the setting of another sun.

A COLOSSAL JOKE.

URING the peach jubilee at Benton Harbor, Mich., last fall a body of twelve prominent men formed a committee to plan a joke that would stagger the United States and the northern part of Missouri. They advertised that on the last day of the carnival the Hon. Perry Jimpson, of Kansas, would address the people of Benton Harbor. The joke was kept as quiet as a "bone orchard." The committee had no intention of even inviting the Honorable Jimpson to deliver an address. Mr. Steve Bunton, a member of the committee, was sent to Chicago to look up a humorist. He discovered me in my office, which is on Clark street under an awning. He told me of the committee's plan and how it expected to carry out the joke to a successful end. He said the object of his trip to Chicago was presumably on business, but ostensibly to hire me to impersonate Perry Jimpson in an address to what was expected to be one of the largest crowds that Benton Harbor had ever held. He wanted to know if I had ever made a political speech. I told him that was just where I was at home. I had stumped seven different states for seven different parties. I was never on the winning side, however, but I made the speeches just the same. He allowed that I could fill the bill and named the amount set aside for a joke of that size. I accepted his offer.

On his return to Benton Harbor he reported his success to the other members of the committee and Jimpson day was thoroughly advertised. The daily papers boomed the coming of the distinguished man, although the editors were ignorant of the joke. This was not right, however, as the newspaper men should have been at the head of the committee. There is no use to try to keep a secret from the newspapers. It may be hidden for a time, but sooner or later they will get you sure. The committee advertised half-fare on all railroads. Everything was moving along just about right and the prospects for a big crowd were good.

Mr. Bunton kept up a continual correspondence with me to satisfy himself, as well as the other members of the committee, that I would not disappoint them.

I had never seen the Honorable Jimpson, and did not know what kind of a looking man he was. Neither did I know to a certainty what political principle he advocated.

I set about to look up his political career. All this I found. He had been sent to congress three times and had lived long enough to be seventeen years older than I am. I also learned that he was not hoseless, but a club gentleman, a man of letters, dignified, learned, cultured and could dally with philosophy and rhetoric like our old high school chum—Socrates. All this for a moment caused me to weaken on the impersonation which I had promised to give, as it is difficult for a man who only runs about seventeen in deportment to impersonate another who has his walls plastered with sheepskins.

My first dress rehearsal was in trying to look seventeen years older. I sprouted a full growth of whiskers about ten days long, which resembled pin feathers more than anything else.

I BOWED LOW TO THAT GREAT MULTITUDE.

The dreaded day came at last. Mr. A. M. Gammond, one of the members of the committee, was sent to Chicago to meet the Honorable Jimpson and escort him to Benton Harbor. When he met me he was very liberal with his compliments on my makeup. I had my hair and pin feathers painted an iron gray. I wore eye glasses and walked something like a before taking patent liver medicine advertisement. This was no reflection on Mr. Jimpson, but I assumed the look in order to appear old enough. I wore a tight hacking cough and a cane to complete the makeup.

Mr. Gammond asked me on the train if I was subject to stage fright or thought I would get nervous. I told him there was no backwardness in my makeup, as any man who was brave enough to live through two winters' in Chicago could go to Africa, fight lions in the jungles, then marry a lady barber on his return.

In due time the train rolled into the station. About 2,000 people were waiting to welcome the hero of the day. Carriages were lined up on all sides. The brass band struck up with that familiar march, "George Washington." As I stepped off the car Mr. Gammond introduced me to the entire committee and I was shown the carriage in waiting where I took my seat with other celebrities. As the procession, headed by a band, started over the line of march hundreds of people on both sides of the street sent up loud cheers of welcome. I bowed low to that great multitude and showed my appreciation for their cordial reception. When our carriage stopped at the Hotel Benton, the reception committee escorted me to my quarters. All eyes were upon me. For once in my life I had the extreme pleasure of feeling that I was a great man; a man of notoriety and a brainy speaker. After hurried introductions to some of Benton Harbor's pleasant citizens, I was led to the scaffold, or rather a temporary platform in front of the hotel. Mr. Gammond's brother had the honor of introducing me to 20,000 people as the speaker of the day. I may say here that he knows how to introduce men of note. I was greeted with deafening applause which lasted for two minutes. As well as I can remember part of my speech ran as follows:

"Fellow Citizens and Political Friends: Allow me to thank you for the enthusiastic reception and the high honor which you have bestowed upon me, in inviting me to address you on this occasion. When the invitation was read at my home in Kansas (that was a lie, I never saw Kansas), I assure you that it was with pride that I accepted."

"Gosh all fish hooks that feller looks tarnation young for Perry," I heard an old farmer remark. Then I assumed the look of the liver medicine advertisement.

"My friends, with all your tireless preparation, the presence of such a vast gathering of people and the glad hand of welcome to your city is overwhelming."

(Applause and cries of louder! from the tops of buildings and telegraph poles.)

"I have been in many countries (that's another) and I have seen many orchards of fruit, but I am frank to confess that here at your festival you have the finest exhibition of early rose peaches that ever grew."

"You are right, Perry, that's no josh. Three cheers for Jimpson," came from the audience.

"There is no reason why you should not have the finest, because you have the soil, because you have the climate, because you are industrious, because you are not afraid of work and because you are ambitious and made of the right kind of timber."

Sickening applause cries of "louder" and "down in front."

"Now, my friends, I want to say a few words to you on a matter of very grave importance. Do you know that in your very midst there is lurking a mighty blood-sucking vampire? You have been taught from the cradle that you are living in a land of liberty. It will not long be so if you do not respect your vote as you would a prayer to your Creator. This vampire I speak of is hour by hour and inch by inch crawling upon you to rob you of your homes and liberty. I have reference to the trusts formed during this administration."

Applause loud and long.

"Think well, fellow citizens, think well, at the next election before you cast your vote. You should be as careful with your vote as you are with your peach crop. If you do not raise it as you should, that is your fault. If you do not vote as you should, that is also your fault, and the time will come when combinations will raise you clear off your homestead. (Thundering applauses.)

* * * * * * * *

"In conclusion permit me to say a few words on the American banking system. In the first place no bank has a right to fail only by an act of God Almighty. I have a hundred fold more confidence in a three ball shop than I have in a bank. You can force them to deal honestly with you, but you can not a bank. You will notice that every time a bank fails a sign will go up on the door: 'Closed on account of inability to realize on securities.' Right then and there the officers of that bank should go to prison for life and if they tried to plead not guilty, the judge should give them twenty years more. (Great applause.)

"In my mind the Chinese have the proper banking system. There has been but one bank failure in that country in 500 years. In case of a failure there they cut off the heads of the officials. I thank you for your attention."

The conclusion was received with loud cheers and hip, hip, hurrahs, for Jimpson.

The two papers of the town did not go to press until I had finished my address. One had a stock picture of Coxey which it ran with the following comment:

"Jimpson is here. Talked five minutes and told all he knew. Said nothing and crowd sold."

When Mr. Gammond read that he said he thought it best for me to return to Chicago and not spoil the joke. I did not care so much about spoiling the joke; I was afraid some one might spoil me. So to bring about a comfortable feeling I got out of there for Chicago on the first train.

This happened eleven months ago and I understand the papers are roasting that committee yet. The funniest part of the story is—it's the truth.

BONDING THE COUNTY.

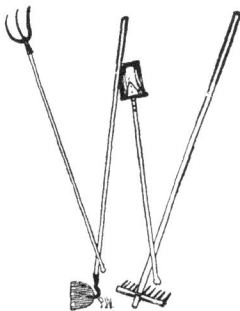

HEN Washington county, Ark., was bonded for a railroad a mighty howl went up from every old settler around Persimmon Ridge and Possum Bottom. They were bitterly opposed to one of those "pesky" railroads "spilin'" the farms in that county. With all the protests, somehow, the road went through.

Some time after that a report broke loose from its hitching place and took the rounds that Benton county was also about to be bonded for a railroad. The farmers entered a protest at once.

Ezra Tunson was the county road supervisor at Bentonville. He was a true type of the men in that section of Arkansaw. He always wore a bunch of oakum on his chin, which is not out of place in that state. No one ever saw him when he did not have his mouth filled with long green tobacco, unless some one offered him "store boughten," which he never had the heart to refuse. He had a pronounced individuality. When he expectorated bystanders got out of the way. His chewing was his own style and reminded one of a lively tobacco worm. He wore butternut trousers, one leg of which hung over the strap of his boot. They were held in place by a bed tick gallus. The connection was made by means of a hickory peg or a four-penny nail; he allowed that was good enough. If he disliked anyone he would never grant them the smallest favor. One of his neighbors, for whom he never had much use because he fought in the Union army, said to him one day:

"Ezra, got any chawin' terbacker?"

"Nope," said he; "but I got some uv the all-firedest best rosum that you ever stuck a tooth in."

On account of Ezra holding the office of road supervisor the farmers all looked up to him with much respect. On any Saturday afternoon he could be seen on some street corner in Bentonville with a crowd around him discussing the evils of railroads. No matter what he said the listeners all reckoned that Ezra was right about it.

After much talk they decided to hold a grievance meeting at the Elm Creek schoolhouse. When the meeting opened every bench in the house was filled and there wasn't even standing room. Ezra being the phosphorescent gleam of that section, was of course called upon to speak first. He took his corner, grabbed his bunch of oakum, spit over his chin and started to speak.

"Well, gentlemen, I'll tell you," he began by way of introduction. "You kin jist talk all you gosh durned please, but I hain't in favor uv bondin' this here county fur a railroad. Now thar they bonded Washington county fur a road, an' the cussed thing went right through Jim Jones's farm, right 'twixt the smokehouse an' the corn crib, an' dog my buttons if that d—— fool dog of Jim's didn't run hisse'f clean to death after that confounded train. That wuz the fust thoroughbreed dog that ever hit the state. He had a pedigree as long as a fence rail, an' fetlocks ten inches long. Besides the train went right through the woods an jarred all the acorns of'en the trees and starved every razor back to death from Pea Ridge to Cross Hollows. An' the same train hit Bill Evans' bay steer in the hind quarters of his

"HE HAD A PEDIGREE AS LONG AS A FENCE RAIL, AN' FET-
LOCKS TEN INCHES LONG."

system an' knocked 'em clean into White river, an' I'll be hanged if I'm in favor uv bondin' this here county."

With this Ezra let go of another collection of long green juice and almost put out the fire in the stove, then he took his seat.

The next speaker was Cy Willard. He was very timid, as it was his first appearance:

"AN' THE SAME TRAIN HIT BILL EVANS' BAY STEER IN THE HIND QUARTERS OF HIS SYSTEM AN' KNOCKED 'EM CLEAN INTO WHITE RIVER."

"Feller voters of this here township, I want to tell you. I'm a man uv a few words an' I'm through talkin.' "

He took his seat and the meeting adjourned.

MARK ANTHONY.

BRUTUS was a shrewd ward politician; and if alive today would without doubt be a chronic candidate for president of the United States. After the murder of Cæsar he entreated the citizens to allow him to depart alone. He asked them to kindly stay and hear Mark Anthony's speech. We will picture these citizens as a gang of tough Bowery politicians, and Anthony as a clever ward heeler, and the smoothest talker that ever took out his second papers. And we will say that his speech was delivered yesterday and it all happened in the following modern style:

1st Cit. "Say fellers! come on and stick for de big show, see? Markey, old boy, is goin' to give us a speil."

2nd Cit. "Take de scaffold, Markey, an' don't get gay wid your kiddin'."

3rd Cit. "Dat's right; if de guy gets fresh we'll t'row 'im in de sweat-house, see?"

Ant. "For Casey's sake I am beholding to you."

4th Cit. "What did de dub say 'bout Casey?"

2nd Cit. "Oh, I don't know; somethin' 'bout holdin' 'im up. If de guy says Casey ain't on de square, we'll soak 'im one, eh fellers?"

94

1st Cit.   "Yes, an' dat's no jolly."

Ant.   "Friends, politicians, countrymen, lend me your ears."

3rd Cit.   "Ah, lend yez nothin'; do yer t'ink we're a tree ball game?"

"FOR CASEY'S SAKE I AM BEHOLDING TO YOU."

1st Cit.   "Well, I should say nit; not on yer life."

Ant.   "I come to bury O'Malley, not to praise him. The evils that men do live after them; the good is oft interred with their bones.   So let it be with O'Malley.

The noble Casey hath told you O'Malley was ambitious. If it were so, it was a grevious fault; and greviously hath O'Malley answered it. Here under leave of Casey and the rest (for Casey is an honorable man; so are they all, all honorable men)."

1st Cit. "Yes, and dat ain't no kid. De hull bunch of dem fellers is honorable guys, see? Da ain't a bad oyster in de push."

Ant. "Come I to speak in O'Malley's funeral. He was my friend, faithful and just to me. But Casey says, he was ambitious; and Casey is an honorable man."

4th Cit. "Ah, yer said dat before Markey. 'Course Casey is all right. He is de wisest guy on de Bowery."

Ant. "He hath brought captives home to New York whose ransoms did the general coffers fill. Did this in O'Malley seem ambitious? When that the poor have cried, O'Malley hath wept: Ambition should be made of sterner stuff. Yet Casey says, he was ambitious; and Casey is an honorable man."

2nd Cit. "Say Markey, cut out dat chewin' 'bout Casey's honor, or we'll tump yez in de troat, see?"

Ant. "You all did see that on the Lupercal—"

3rd Cit. "Who's de tart he's talkin' 'bout—Lou Percal?"

1st Cit. He's got me skinned, Mickie; I don't know her."

Ant. "I thrice presented him a kingly crown, which he did thrice refuse. Was this ambitious? Yet Casey says he was ambitious; and sure, he is an honorable man."

1st Cit. "Say, Markey, if yez don't chop on dat guff 'bout Casey we'll hand yez an upper cut dat yer can't block, see?"

3rd Cit. "Wonder what kinder dope his royaletts has been smokin', eh?"

Ant. "I speak not to disprove what Casey spoke, but here I am to speak what I do know. You all did love him once, not without cause; what cause withholds you then to mourn for him? O, judgment, thou art fled to brutish beasts. And men have lost their reason! Bear with me, my heart is in the coffin with O'Malley, and I must pause 'till it comes back to me."

1st Cit. "Say fellers, maybe de guy is givin' it to us on de square."

4th Cit. "I guess O'Malley had de hooks trown into 'im and got de worst of it."

* * * * * * * *

Ant. "If you have tears, prepare to shed them now. You all do know this Prince Albert. I remember the first time ever O'Malley put it on. 'Twas on a summer's evening, in his tenement house. That day he overcame the Hoolahans. Look! in this place ran Sullivan's dagger through; see what a rent the envious Hogan made."

1st Cit. "Well, dat's all right, Markey, why didn't de big stiff pay his rent, eh?"

2nd Cit. Oh, quit your kiddin' fellers, Markey is givin' us de right steer. See? He's got me on de run, and it's no pipe."

4th Cit. "Come on, all of yez, and we'll go down to de fort ward and chew up every cheap guy dat had a hand in puttin' out O'Malley's light, see?"

LACERATED ASPIRATIONS.

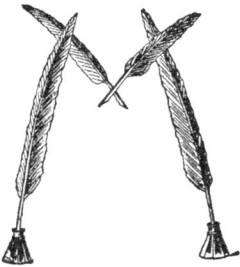

Y FOLKS used to say they knew from the way I put curls on my capital letters that some day I would be a newspaper man. I had the side of the barn and all the fences around the place covered with capital letters made with the full arm movement. After I grew old enough to work out my road tax I tried my hand at story writing. The first story—as well as I can remember—was something about:

"When the potato winked its eye and the cabbage bowed its head."

It was a sort of vegetable courtship anyway. I sent that story to the Portland Oregonian. I received a letter from the editor and he said since I had not enclosed stamps for the return of the manuscript he had sent same to the business manager and requested me to correspond with him. This I did. He wrote me that he had scanned the story and would publish it for $23. I was anxious to see my name and story in print and the money was promptly sent. On account of a grave mistake on the part of some one in the business office, my story was run twice. I heard afterward that the mistake cost the paper 1,200 subscribers.

I then went to Seattle, Wash., and called at the office of the Post Intelligencer. By telling the editor a lot of stuff about myself that could not be proven in a court of justice I was put to work. My first assignment was

I TRIED MY HAND AT STORY WRITING.

easy. I was sent to report a pink tea party which was to be given by a Mrs. J. Henry Walters. I did the best I could and wrote it up, as I thought, about right. Unfortunately for me the proof reader made an unpardon-

able error.   The story was printed as I wrote it except
one word.   It read:

"A delightful time, etc., at Mrs. Walter's 'punk' tea
party."

I DID NOT KNOW WHAT HE WANTED, BUT I SOON FOUND OUT.

The editor sent for me and then told me the book-
keeper wanted to speak to me.   I did not know what
he wanted, but I soon found out.   He simply said:

"The boss told me to separate you from your earnings."

I then went to Spokane. When I arrived The Daily Review was the first paper in my mind. I told the editor that I was a reporter and had worked all over the country. He employed me at once. The first assignment there was to write up the county fair. In making the rounds of the fair I noticed a beautiful painting. I gave some little space to this remarkable piece of art, painted with a deft hand, etc., by a Mrs. M. F. Warren. I turned in my copy in due time with my soul filled with hope that my style of writing would please the editor. As luck would have it the proof reader again got in his deadly work. The story read:

"A remarkable piece of art, etc., by Mrs. M. F. Warren, which she painted with her 'left' hand."

The editor told me that he was sorry, but the book-keeper was waiting for me down stairs.

RIDING A BULL CALF.

ROTHER BILL was seven years older than me, but in any dangerous adventures I always took the lead. Not because I wanted to, but be-because of his orders. Pa was op-posed to us riding calves on the Sab-bath day, or any other day for that matter. When he told us not to do a thing we obeyed him—some-times.

We had one calf that I had fed and cared for from the time it was a suckling. We planned to break it to the saddle at the first oppor-tunity. It soon came. Early one Sunday morning pa told us to hitch up for meeting. We put some straw and five or six raw-hide bottom chairs in the wagonbed. Bill winked at me and I winked at him, for we knew we would have to stay at home and take care of things. In due time every member of the family—except Bill and I—was on the road to the Ebenezer meeting house to hear the new preacher. Bill said:

"I was just thinking that on account of you being so much lighter than me, you had better take the first ride."

I did not object as I knew it was useless. We soon had that calf looking like a war horse. He was equipped with a blind bridle and a U. S. army saddle. Bill helped me to mount and to be sure that the calf did not lose me, he tied my feet together under his belly. Up to this time the calf had raised no objections. He was as meek as a lamb, and stood chewing his cud.

"Are you ready?" Bill asked.

I told him I was all ready but that I didn't know whether the calf was or not. I asked Bill to give the calf a punch with a fence rail and see if he would start. That was tried but it did not work. Then Bill tried to start him by prodding him with a long stick, but it was no use.

"Get up there!" Bill yelled, but the calf made no reply.

I then suggested to Bill that he twist the calf's tail. That was a happy thought for Bill, but not for me. The moment Bill took a twist on his tail he let out a sickening bawl and went into the air about seven feet, kind of rainbow fashion, and came down stiff-legged. I would not have thought so much about one of those trips in the air, but the air habit seemed to grow on the calf and he spent half his time off the ground. When he did light each time I was sorry, as I was sure to lose a suspender and a lot of buttons.

All this time he was headed for Texas, or at least in that direction, at a high rate of speed. About every forty feet he would let out that bawl and then take the aerial flight. Ahead of us for two miles was a worm fence built along the roadside, with a number of peach trees scattered along in the fence corners. I saw Mr. Wilson coming down the road with a mule and a cow hitched to his wagon. He had my sympathy, for I knew if he did not get out on one side we would run into him and it would take the neighbors an hour to pick up his wreck. Fortunately he discovered that the calf was running away and he left the road. When we passed him he could not tell whether I was a boy or a dummy, for by this time the calf had bucked most of my clothing off me. On and on we went until a bunch of sand shoats

HE LET OUT A SICKENING BAWL AND WENT INTO THE AIR
ABOUT SEVEN FEET.

jumped out of a fence corner terror stricken. This gave the calf a new start. He went into the air higher than ever and when he lighted the string with which my feet were tied broke and I went into the air alone. I came down in the forks of a peach tree. That was the last I remembered. When pa was returning from the meeting house he discovered a strange boy in that tree. He put me in the wagon, while all the folks looked on

I CAME DOWN IN THE FORKS OF A PEACH TREE.

with pity. When they reached home and brought me back to life so I could speak they found out that I was their youngest son. Father advertised and offered a reward for the calf, but he was never heard of afterward.

FIRST APPEARANCE.

A PAIR of humorists rained into Spokane one day for the purpose of making people laugh. They lectured at the Auditorium and I went to hear them. I thought well of their humor, and several times it was all I could do to keep my face straight. I thought I could be quite as funny if I had a chance.

Shortly after that I went to the manager of the opera house and asked him what it would cost for his play house per night.

"What do you want with it?" was his stagey answer.

"I want to lecture there," I replied.

"On what subject?"

"Wit and Humor."

"What do you take for it?"

"For wit I will take the stage, for humor I can take Hive syrup."

"Do you know the present price of eggs?"

"I am not joking. I mean business," I replied with dignity.

"Whom do you suppose would attend your lecture?" he sneeringly asked.

"I do not know. I just want to try my hand and see if I can make a hit."

"Are you aware of the fact that an audience can sometimes make a 'hit' and not take the stage either?"

"I do not mind that, as I have arranged for an armor."

I AM NOT JOKING. I MEAN BUSINESS.

"Well, if you mean business, I will let you have the opera house for $150."

"I guess you misunderstand me. I do not care to become a stockholder in the house; I just want to rent it 'or one night."

"Very well then, since it's only to be a lecture and you will not require the stage hands, you may have it for $100."

I made him promise to stand in the wings of the stage the night of the lecture and after it was over to criticise me honestly, and tell me what he thought of my humor.

I billed the town for ten days with yellow posters. The night came, the great asbestos drop curtain went up and I bowed low to a fair sized audience of smiling faces. They were not smiling at the funny things that they expected to hear, but at my nerve in making my first appearance in my own town. I met quite a number of my friends the next day, but they made no mention of the lecture pro or con. I concluded that they did not like to discourage me.

I went to the opera house manager and asked him what he thought of my style of talk. He said:

"Well, I don't know exactly, but if you want an honest criticism from me, I would advise you never to lecture in the same place twice."

I asked the proprietor of the Daily Evening Chronicle—on which paper I was employed at the time—if he would allow me to report my lecture. He said he would. This saved me, as I took the opportunity to smear encomiums all over my debut. I have never had such a chance since. With this panegyrized press notice I felt safe in making a tour of the country. I could not afford to employ an advance agent, so I decided to go to a town and hire a boy to go up and down the streets ringing a bell, and at the same time give the alarm that I was to lecture that night at a certain hall.

My first appearance after leaving Spokane was in Wenatche. There was no hall in that place and I had to use the dining room of the hotel. I do not know why, but the audience there seemed to be very obtuse, as there was no applause. The only way that I could give them light on the subject was to set a barn on fire.

I left that place for Puget Sound. I may say here with pride, that I have talked longer to one audience than any man living. Eight days and nights on the same subject, and no one left me. It was in a Pullman car in the Cascade Mountains, on the Great Northern Railroad. We were snowbound and could not get out until the snow plough came to our rescue.

When I arrived in Everett, I soon completed arrangements to lecture under the wing of the Methodist Church. The night of the show was a stormy one. I sat in the church very much discouraged, waiting for some one to come in. It seemed to me more like a frost than a rainstorm. At about 8:30 o'clock I heard the ring of silver at the door. The rain had abated and the people were coming in. They kept on coming; men, women and children. My heart grew lighter. On and on they came, until the church was packed to the doors. I never felt in better shape to get funny. I made a rough guess to myself that it must be a $200 house at least. I lectured on the history of my past life; it was the funniest thing I could think of. I talked for an hour and eighty minutes. When it was all over and the audience had gone, I went to the doorkeeper with a smile.

"We had a full house tonight," I remarked.

"Oh, yes, a large one for this town. I think this church never held so many people before at one time."

"I feel complimented, I assure you. How much did you take in?"

"Let's see—the receipts are $4.75."

"Why, how is that? The church was filled with people, and I calculated that it would be a $200 house at least."

"Well, you see, most everyone here tonight belongs to this church, and I did not think it was right to charge them admission."

I had been told that there were ups and downs in the business. I did not complain to this generous hearted doorkeeper; I just moved on to North Yakima the next day. I was told there that it was positively of no use to give a show in that place, as the people were too hard up. A panic had hit the town and there wasn't a dollar in circulation. There wasn't anything left. Wall paper was not used any longer. The people had their houses papered and plastered with mortgages. I found out that the only way I could get a crowd to hear me, was to take vegetables. For the novelty of it I advertised my lecture thus:

"Money not wanted. Come out and see 'A Bundle of Sunshine.' Bring your children; they will enjoy it. Also bring along some farm produce. I will enjoy that. I am easy to please and I hope you will be."

I played to a crowded house. The farmers came in from all directions loaded down with vegetables. They seemed to appreciate my talk very much. Some of them were so enthusiastic that they playfully tossed up some early garden stuff to me while I was on the stage. They were an honest lot of farmers and wanted to be sure that I got what was coming to me. Of course they could have handed the vegetables to me in a quiet way or left them with the doorkeeper, but they had lived so long in the far west fighting Indians and chasing coyotes that a habit of throwing things had grown upon them.

I CALCULATED THAT IT WOULD BE A $200 HOUSE AT LEAST.

III

I carried out the program as advertised. When the
audience had departed I carried out a sack of flour.

The next place in which I showed was Pasco. There
I put up a wire fence between the audience and the stage

THEY PLAYFULLY TOSSED UP SOME EARLY GARDEN STUFF TO
ME WHILE I WAS ON THE STAGE.

for self protection. It was the only thing I furnished
them with that they could see through and not throw
through.

Three days afterward I landed in Mount Idaho. I went to the only hotel in the town and asked the land-lord if he could let me have a room.

"No, sir, I am full," he said.

"I hope you will pardon me, sir, but your face shows it," I sedately replied.

He told me the only place he knew of where I could lodge for the night was on a school section of 640 acres two miles east of town. It was court week there and every room was filled. On this account I could not hire a hall. All I could do was to book myself for the next season. Through idle curiosity I went to the court room and listened to the district attorney exam-ine a few farmers for the purpose of testing their quali-fications as jurors. One man was quite deaf, I remem-ber, and the attorney said to him:

"Sike Raymond is your name, I believe?"

"Which?"

"I say, your name is Sike Raymond?"

"Yes, sir."

"Where do you live, Mr. Raymond?"

"How?"

"Where do you live?"

"I live over on Salmon River."

"Do you know anything about this case?"

"What say?"

"I say, do you know anything about this case?"

"Well, judge, I don't think I know enough about it to act as one of the jurymen."

"I believe you are a little deaf, are you not?"

"Beg pardon."

"You are somewhat deaf, I believe?"

"Yes, sir."

"To what extent are you deaf?"

"Little louder, please."

"I say, to what extent are you deaf?"

"Well, sir, by the wagon road I think it must be about thirty miles."

I went to Grangeville from there and soon arranged for a night of mirth-making. I had to play to such a small house that the show was forced to disband the next day. The reason I say disband, is because it sounds better than dis-strand-ed.

The stagecoach line out of there did not do a credit business and it worked a hardship on the one man drama. I left my scenery in Grangeville and started home. It took me five weeks to make the trip. Even the old settlers claimed that the roads had not been in so bad a condition in twenty years.

A SERMON.

R. R. F. M. ANDREWS, the man who wrote: "Who Put Glue in Father's Whiskers," "The Ossified Man Died Hard," "A Splinter from My Sweetheart's Wooden Leg," "Did Her Switch Match Her Hair," "Come Where My Love Lies Dreaming—and Get Shot," "Your Necktie is Up in the Back," "Who Will Crack Ice for Pa's Gout," "Grandma's Corns are Soaked in Oil," and a hundred other popular songs for five cents, has caused me more trouble than any other man west of Buffalo. He came to me one bright spring morning with the country fever. He wanted to go to the country at once and spend the summer and nothing would do but I must go along. We started for Green Bay, Wis., and succeeded in getting there.

We called upon Mr. Jenkins, editor of The Daily Advocate, and asked him if he wanted to hire two bright, energetic, sober newspaper men. He said he could use a couple of good men for a while, but would want some reference. We told him that was easy. I referred him to Mr. Andrews for my reference, and Mr. Andrews referred him to me for his reference. Although Mr.

Jenkins had never heard of either of us, he was well
satisfied with the references furnishd.   He said:

"Now, of course, you will find the work on a country
daily very different from that of a big city daily.   You

"THERE WILL BE WOOD TO SAW FOR THE STOVES."

will have to solicit subscribers and advertisements.   At
times you can make yourselves useful in the composing
room.   There will be wood to saw for the stoves.   Besides you can help around the house on wash days and
at house cleaning time you can beat the carpets and

paper the rooms. Sometimes the folks go to the theater, then you will be expected to wash the supper dishes. You can also get all the news around town, write some of the editorials, make up the paper, and when we are short on boys you can take a route and help out with the delivery. There are also two cows to milk. This work you can do turn about."

We accepted the position and started in. We both took department columns. Mr. Andrews always headed his column thus: "With the Colonel," and mine was: "With the Yardmaster." Mr. Andrews was educated for a minister of the gospel. He did not follow the business very long, as he was a firm believer in Sunday closing. In his department he always wrote a Sunday morning sermon, while my department was devoted to local events. He had a habit of leaving town very often and asking me to write his column, which I did willingly. One day he took a notion to visit the Soo. He said he would be away over Sunday and would like to have me write his sermon, milk the cows and feed his dog. I told him to go ahead, I would attend to the sermon. On Sunday morning the following sermon appeared:

"Dearly beloved: The theme of my discourse will be found in the eighth verse of the second chapter of Genesis.

"'And the Lord planted a garden eastward in Eden, and there he put the man whom he had formed.'

"Let me invite your attention to a lone man in the garden of Eden. He was put there for a purpose. Put there to pull weeds and keep the briars and poison oak cut down.

"Now this man's name was Adam. He was extremely reticent and very conservative; being the only person on earth he had but little to say. There was no other

living being to argue or pick a fuss with him. He had
a clear title to the garden of Eden. He mapped out his
future in which he could see nothing but whole quarter
sections of happiness. He had an apple orchard of yellow bell flowers and newtown pippins that would make
an orchard of this day and time look like seedlings. He
did not have to go to work by the whistle nor did he
have to listen to the tintinnabulum of curfew. Then
there was the land of Havaliah which was far richer in
gold than the Klondyke. All he had to do was to turn
the Pison river on it and go to work. What more could
he ask for? And yet I say, why should he trouble
himself about work? No doubt the sight of gold would
have excited him, and greed for much gold would have
broken in upon his happiness.

"Why should he do that which might mar his days
of peace? He had every gift that man could ask. He
could kick his breakfast off some choice fruit tree. The
climate was perfect and his bed was made of roses and
he used the canopy of heaven for his counterpanes. The
first bad break he made was neglecting to build a high
picket fence around that tree of knowledge. Of course
he had never thought of anyone else getting him into
a mixup over that tree, as he owned the earth and had
no one to keep away from the tree but himself. He
should have had forethought enough, however, to sus-
pect that sooner or later some one would come along
and break up his syndicate. Think, my friends, what
a life of peace and perfect bliss he could have lived had
he not been interrupted.

"During that deep sleep of his little did he dream of
losing one of his ribs. Little did he know the trouble
it would bring him, and little did he dream that one
of his own ribs would appear unto him in the form of

a woman without clothing and claim him as her husband. Right there and then she set up a howl for a new dress, and the women folks have been howling for something to wear ever since. Of course Adam had not been to the tailors himself, but he was on earth first and had a right to adopt a makeup to suit his own fancy. He had never even thought of touching the forbidden fruit in the garden, but just as soon as Eve found out there was such a tree she couldn't sleep until she knew all about how it happened—hence the breaking up of Adam's happy home. As to the subtility of the serpent, it is safe to presume that was simply one of Eve's subterfuges. In my mind the serpent was not guilty. Eve felt happy when she got Adam to eat some of the fruit, as she thought he would help her lay the blame on the serpent, when the time came to give an account of the affair. The result of the whole thing was, Adam and the snake got the worst of it.

"Adam no longer had a squatter's claim on the garden of Eden. He had to leave behind the only fruit bearing orchard on earth, all on account of this woman. It was a fine piece of property to fall into the hands of Cherubims. He was forced to return to the land of his birth and follow the plough all the rest of his days. Had Eve not been so curious there would have been a different story to tell. Besides she established a bad precedent, which has ever kept womankind excited with curiosity.

"In conclusion, brethren, let me say that happiness is all you want. If your garden of Eden is cut down and taken from you, I say unto you, be not aggrieved. Grab the plough handles of unrest and get across the field of life as best you can. Amen."

The next day Mr. Andrews returned from the Soo.
After he read the sermon he asked me to hold his hat
while he had a fit.   He declared I had ruined him.

HE SAID MOST OF THE SUBSCRIBERS HAD STOPPED THEIR PAPER.

"Why!" he said, "that is a sacrilege!   It is the most
irreverent thing I ever heard and both of us will lose
our heads."   Sure enough Mr. Jenkins sent for us.   He
said most of the subscribers had stopped their paper
and the only way that the paper could live was to change
it from a daily to a weekly, which was done that day.

He told us that the bookkeeper wanted to see us, which he did. We were again out in the cold world. I told Andrews we could go to some other place and soon get work, as we could furnish references. He felt a little consoled by what I said. He quoted a passage of Scripture: "Sufficient unto the day is the evil thereof." I said: "You are right about that; and, besides, there are no pockets in a shroud."

LALLA ROOKH'S DESCENDANT.

I HAVE never held a position long for I hate the eternal monotony of life. I have never traveled a trail without finding it full of stones and ruts. I have found obstructions in all the walks of life. My progress has been greatly impeded. I may look afar and see a green, shady woodland, and wish for just one hour there, that I might stroll around and commune with wild grape vines, cowslips and he ferns. But I dare not go, as I know the poison ivy flourishes there and that is my enemy. If anyone speaks of that vine in my presence my face swells up like a poisoned feline.

If I undertake to lecture there is sure to be a Democratic rally or a fire. In such a case I had just as well be talking under the auspices of a Minnesota blizzard. My success would amount to the same in either case.

When I lectured in Iowa and Kansas my advance agent was a cyclone. When Coxey got on the warpath his army headed me off in every town between Seattle and Washington, D. C. When I followed the plough it was not an uncommon thing to strike an elm root and break a trace and at the same time have the root fly back and hit me on the shin.

I have gone home at night when the day's work was done and an expert harness maker could not have guessed for what my traces were meant. Every time they broke I would have to repair them with whatever material I might have handy. They were made up of pieces of chain, hickory withes, cotton rope, papaw bark, fence wire and some leather. I spent my evening setting up with my shins and thinking of the next day's flirtation with those traces, elm roots and a plough mule that had an embodiment of colossal cheek and a plaintive smile that meant no good. A mule will look pleasant for four years just to draw one on so it can get a real good chance to kick him clean out of debt.

When the United States declared war with Spain I wanted to enlist as a chaplain, but someone told my past history and I was rejected.

I was once lost in the mountains of Josephine county, Oregon, for seven days, during which time it seemed to me I had traveled 700 miles. The mental agony I suffered can never be told. You might sit and listen to a sad story for a month, told by some one who had been lost, and you could not begin to imagine what torture that person had to suffer. I climbed over high mountains and descended into deep canyons. The nights were as black as ink, and the frightening cries of wolves and coyotes were enough to drive me mad. Lost! forever lost! was the only thought that ran through my brain. On the evening of the seventh day I came to a trail, but I could see no signs of anyone having passed over it for months. I was exhausted and compelled to stop. I dropped down in my tracks and fell asleep. I felt and believed that it would be the long sleep of death that comes to all, sooner or later.

The night wore on while fiendish dreams set fire to my brain. It was the first time in the seven days that I had closed my eyes. I heard the voices of wild beasts; I saw a thousand devils come up out of the sea. The world was fast being destroyed. Great volcanoes belched melted stones high into the air. A terrific storm was raging. The loud claps of thunder shook the earth and the lightning set the forests on fire. The heavens were open and the deep gorges below me were filling up with a mighty flood, crashing down trees and cutting away the mountain sides with a deafening roar as it rushed on into an unknown region. I saw no escape, for on every side there was destruction. I felt the earth below me quiver. I saw great cracks in the crust swallowing up huge trees. The fissures were rapidly widening and I knew the spot where I rested would soon be a great lake of boiling stones and forests. I felt something shake me. I awoke and two men stood before me in the light of the morning sun. They were trappers who happened along that trail and found me more dead than alive.

For seven days I did not have a morsel to eat except some dried salmon. From that day to this I have never looked a fish in the face.

In Walla Walla, Washington, I once secured employment in a soap factory. My duty was to stand on top of a deep vat with one foot on one side and one on the other, and stir the batch. One day my right foot slipped and I fell into the hot soap up to my waist. A fellow worker dragged me out and for many days after that I was busy in a hospital growing together.

When I was a boy I was unhappy unless I was imitating something. I remember once I climbed a tree and walked out on one of its branches to show some

boys how I could imitate a blue jay. The first thing
a blue jay does when he lights is to turn completely
around, then he wipes his face on the limb and takes
another turn around. I made the announcement to the

I AWOKE AND TWO MEN STOOD BEFORE ME IN THE LIGHT OF
THE MORNING SUN.

boys, that I would jump high enough to clear the limb
and turn around. I jumped high enough and turned completely around, but I did not light just like a blue jay.
My feet missed the limb and it caught me under the

chin. The earth's gravity was too strong for me and
I struck on the ground head first. When they picked
me up my collar bone was broken and my imitating
season closed.

MY RIGHT FOOT SLIPPED AND I FELL INTO THE HOT SOAP UP
TO MY WAIST.

I was once told to eat bird seed and cuttle fish if I
would be a good singer. I tried it. If the doctor had
not been handy I might have been a good singer, but
not on this earth.

I took the dogs out one day for a rabbit hunt. It was not long until I heard the bark of old Tige. He had something up a hollow tree. I cut a long hazel twig and split the end of it so I could twist the animal

MY FEET MISSED THE LIMB AND IT CAUGHT ME UNDER THE CHIN.

out. I worked for sometime before I could get a good hold on its fur. I gave a steady pull and out it came. The dogs did not run up to help me, but went the other way. I soon backed out myself, as it was not my kind

of a rabbit.   It had a bushy tail and white stripes down
it's back.   When I returned home the folks would not
allow me to come into the house.   I had to stay outside and sleep in straw stacks and corn cribs for a month
after that.   I was as easy to find as a bell cow.

I SOON BACKED OUT MYSELF, AS IT WAS NOT MY KIND OF A
RABBIT.

The first time I was permitted to go hunting alone
with a gun was for me a proud moment.   This gun was
one of those old army muskets.   It would shoot just

as well when loaded with gravel, nails or tacks, as with lead. During my excitement I made the mistake of putting in a double charge of powder, then I went on my way rejoicing. As soon as I reached the hunting

I CAME TO AND FOUND MYSELF ON THE OTHER SIDE OF THE FENCE.

grounds, I saw some chickens flying overhead. As quick as a flash I rested that gun on a fence and fired at those birds. In an hour or so after that I came to and found myself on the other side of the fence. It just then occurred to me that I had heard an uncle of mine say that a musket would kick just as hard as it would shoot.

Hunting wild turkeys by moonlight in the south is a favorite sport.   At the tender age of twelve I tried it.

I TOLD PA HE MUST GET UP AND SEE WHAT A FINE GOBBLER I HAD.

After walking through the woods for several hours one moonlight night I located a roost of these fine birds.   I rested my rifle in the forks of a sapling and took good aim at the object between the moon and myself.   I set

the hind trigger, cocked the hammer and blazed away.
It was a good shot, as I brought down a fine gobbler.
I threw him over my shoulder and started for home as
proud as a boy with his first pair of trousers. It was
very late when I reached home and the family had long
since retired. But that made no difference to me. I
told pa he must get up and see what a fine gobbler r
had. He lighted a candle and came to the door yawn-
ing and rubbing his eyes, and the moment he saw my
bird he said:

"Why! my son, that's not a turkey. It's a buzzard,
and you have violated the law."

The women folks used to give their children sassafras
tea every spring to purify their blood. After a while
they would break out like a Sioux Indian with boil .
They said that' each boil was worth $5. I figured up
my system one spring and found that I was loafing
around with $120 worth of rose-tinted ones. I got i,
the habit of standing up from the first of May unti.
August. If I could have cashed in all the sassafras
boils I had in ten years at $5 each, I could have visited
the old world.

In San Francisco I was hired by a tailoring establish-
ment to act as salesman. I did not know anything about
the business, but I was very willing and meant well.
The first customer who came in the morning I went to
work wanted to select something suitable for a pair of
trousers. He soon found what he wanted. I had noticed a long table in the back end of the store on which
were thirty-six inches marked off to take the place of
a three foot rule as I supposed. I told the customer
to lie down on that table alongside of those inches so
I could take his measure for the trousers. I then got
a yardstick and started in. Just then my employer

came in and saw what I was doing. He let me go without arguing. The next day I coaxed him to hire me over and I would do better. I took a man's measure for a suit and he asked me if we required a deposit. I told him we did, as a big deposit always made a suit fit better. In due time he got his suit and went away. He came into the store a week or two after that and I asked him how his suit fitted him. He said it fitted all right except the coat, pants and vest.

While standing in the door one morning a customer inquired for a misfit suit. I told him that we did not have any on hand just then, but if he would step inside and leave his measure we could make him one by the next evening. My employer overheard the conversation. I tried to prevail upon him to hire me over the third time but it was no use.

In the Esther mines on Grave creek in southern Oregon I rented myself to the mine owners. They used me for a kind of car horse. I ran a dump car in and out of a 300 foot tunnel. I did not mind the work very much, as the track was built so that the car would run out of the tunnel of its own weight, and that gave me a chance to ride. I had to watch the brake closely or the car would run away. The tunnel was almost at the top of a high mountain. At the mouth of the tunnel there was a sharp curve and going around this it was necessary to run slowly to prevent the car leaving the track. One day with a full load of quartz I gave the car a good start and then jumped aboard. When it came time to set the brake it refused to work. The tunnel was not lighted and I could not make up my mind what to do. The speed of the car was increasing every second as the incline was greater near the mouth of the tunnel. I thought of that sharp curve and the

3,000 feet to the bottom of the mountain where a raging river rushed madly on to the sea. On and on that car went toward destruction. At last the curve was reached. The car jumped the track on a high trestle.

I LIGHTED SOMEWHERE FAR BELOW THE CURVE.

The last I remembered was that I was soaring through the air. It was the longest trip I ever made off the earth. I lighted somewhere far below the curve. The car lighted also, but it did not stop until it found a resting place in the bed of the river. When I returned to work I always made sure that the brake was in working order.

The foreman came into the tunnel one morning and upon looking around decided that if he put a blast into the wall at a certain place he might strike a richer vein. There was no trace of gold and very little of silver in the quartz we were working. It ran higher in pig iron than anything else. He took a small drill and held it over his shoulder against the wall of the tunnel and told me to strike it with a sledge. Now I was only a young man and had never struck a drill in my life, and besides the way he stood made the stroke difficult. While I hesitated he gruffly ordered me to strike the drill.

"Do you believe in the efficacy of prayer?" I asked him.

"Never mind your prayer business, you go ahead and strike that drill."

"Is there any word that you would like to send to your folks? The reason I ask you this is because I can foresee that you have not long to live."

"Now if you don't hurry up and strike that drill I'll get some one who can!"

I felt sorry for him, as I knew he did not realize how near to death's door he was standing. I struck the drill very well the first time, but the second time it was not there, or else I missed it, for I hit him a terrific blow in the back and caved in three of his ribs. You can imagine my feelings, as I was sure I had killed him. I called in the miners and we conveyed his mangled form to his cabin.

When he got so he could speak he told the superintendent that if he ever got well he would put out my light. I did not stay around those diggings waiting for him to get well. The climate was bad there anyway.

On the North Umpqua river I stopped one day at a farmer's house and asked him if he had any work for an emigrant boy. He said about all there was to do just at that time was catching driftwood. I thought

·I STRUCK THE DRILL VERY WELL THE FIRST TIME, BUT THE SECOND TIME IT WAS NOT THERE.

of course from the way he spoke that he wanted to hire me and I asked him what wages he was paying for that kind of work.

'Oh, I don't pay wages at all,' he said. "This is

worked on a co-operative plan and it gives you a chance to go into business for yourself, then you can be your own boss.   It is worked like this: You furnish your own boat, hooks and poles, and give me half you catch."

He was known in that section as the Oregon philanthropist.

On the farm I was always told that when a swarm of bees settled on the branch of a tree, or any place for that matter, they could be hived without the least danger, if charmed.   The charming act was done by beating on a tin pan over a hive placed near where they had settled and they would all crawl into the new home.   One day while out in the woods, I discovered a swarm settled on the branch of an oak.   I ran home and told Brother Bill about my find.   He lost no time in getting an old tin pan and a cracker box, and we were off for the place where we could hive a swarm.   Bill told me to climb the tree and take the box with me and he would play the tin pan.   While he was playing what sounded to me like a death march, I crawled out on the branch with the box.   Just then two of the dogs which followed us got into a fight, and Bill dropped the tin pan to separate them.

In the excitement I jarred the limb and dropped the box.   This stirred up the swarm.   They evidently mistook my head for the box, as most of them settled there.   The rest of them took after Bill and the dogs.   I did not go down the tree as I went up.   I just fell out like a wounded owl.   There was a creek near by and I broke for that and fell in head first.   I tried to drown those bees but they still hung on.   I only took my head out of the water long enough to take in some air.   At last I got them off and went home.   It took the folks several days to pull the stingers out of my face and it was nine days before my eyes opened.   It is useless for anyone to speak to me about the busy bees. I know all about them. Just a picture of an apiary is enough. Ever since that time when I hear anyone beating a tin pan I move on.

I DID NOT GO DOWN THE TREE AS I WENT UP.

In the little village of Farmington, Washington, one still night, a burglar came to town and blew open a saloon keeper's safe. No one was disturbed by the explosion. The next morning a crowd of curious citizens gathered in front of the saloon. They talked it over and wondered who the burglar was. They could not imagine who would be so bold as to come into a quiet, peaceful town like Farmington and blow open a safe. I overheard one man say he knew there wasn't a townsman there who would do such a thing. He also suggested that I was the only stranger in town that night. My landlord also heard this and told his waiters that as soon as I left to make a careful invoice of the silverware.

A merchant in Umatilla, Oregon, asked me if I could keep a set of books. I told him I could. He was going to California to spend the winter and he engaged me to look after his accounts. Two months later he returned and inquired how I had been getting along. I told him the very finest. He looked the books through and found that I had never put the scratch of a pen on them. He was more than astonished.

"I thought I hired you to keep this set of books while I was gone," he anxiously remarked.

"Well, I did," I replied.

"I know better; they are just as I left them."

"That I know too; you hired me to keep that set and I did."

"Where and how, for heaven's sake?"

"In my trunk, where no one could bother them."

I am waiting yet for my salary.

I have stumped five different states for five different parties and every candidate I championed was defeated. In 1894 I stumped the state of Montana for the location of the capital at Anaconda. It is needless to say that Anaconda lost and Helena won by 1,900 votes.

I traveled on the road for nine years, during which time I broke up six firms. When I was first sent out I guess I misunderstood the instructions. I thought I was hired to travel and I just traveled. Stopping off at

different towns along the road to sell goods bothered me
but little. I wanted to keep traveling and see the country, and just as long as a firm could stand it I kept on
traveling.

And it has ever been thus through life. So much
thus that I made up my mind last fall while I was in
Buffalo to call on a clairvoyant and get her to dally
with my future. I thought perhaps she could give me
some good advice and get me out of the river of hard
luck and misfortune. I had every reason to remember
my past; all I wanted her to do was to examine my future. Her name was Madam De Blase. I went into
her revelation studio and asked her what she charged.
She replied that her price was fifty cents. I requested
her to roll up her sleeves and go to work. She held my
cold, clammy hand for thirty minutes, all the while telling me what I was and who I was.

"I read in your horoscope that Uranus is in conjunc-
tion with Jupiter," she said with a knitted brow.

"You are a featherless biped and a descendant of
Lalla Rookh. The gentle zephyrs which permeate the
balmy morn are steam heat to you, while they are of
sweetest fragrance to others. You started on the wrong
road in your youth, and the black crags of hard luck tow-
ering high on either side have kept you there ever since.
You will be the sweetheart of loving soubrettes. You will
dally with the queens of tragedy and think for awhile
that your happiness is complete, but not so. It is or-
dained that you be snubbed by a laundress. The nearest
that you will ever come to traveling on a pass will be
when you get permission from some railroad company
to walk over its franchise under a promise that you will
help the section hands do up their chores. Your first
wife's hair will be the color of drug store twine. She

will be very unhappy and your style of providing for her will be the cause of her going back to live with her folks.   Your second wife will have very dark hair, but after she lives with you awhile it will turn red.   She

SHE HELD MY COLD, CLAMMY HAND FOR THIRTY MINUTES.

will be worthy of a good husband, but will soon find out her mistake in taking you for better or for worse.   She will sue you for a divorce on the grounds of non-support.

"I can see by your face that you have a trace of ability. You may yet be in the Halls of Congress—sweeping out and cleaning up. It will be useless for you to ever apply for a position unless they have a cash register, as they will not employ you. You will prosper best among strangers. I could tell you a great deal more but I dislike to offend any one. Fifty cents please."

I paid her and went away. I suppose when the last day comes and I quit this earth I will then find a realm more congenial.

INCONGRUITY.

E ARE taught from childhood never to speak harshly of the dead. A dead person is defenseless, unless a member of a well drilled stock company of spook tragedians. There are few people who will sit through more than one act of a play with spook actors. A spook with a sea green mane and tail feathers can always make a hit in a character part. The audience is generally composed of unwise people who have at some time spoken unkindly of the dead.

This old world is crowded with people who are ever ready to compare a man guilty of some misdeed with an ancient dead offender. I often hear one person refer to another as a bigger liar than Ananias. Now that man died long before Josephus went to Rome to do space work on a morning paper. Taking it for granted that Ananias was in the real estate business and established a bad precedent by not dividing his commissions on a big deal, that is no reason why he should be stigmatized. I have always defended him for this reason: When the fact leaked out that he did not do the square thing, and Peter accused him of willful forgetfulness, he was so grieved that he dropped dead. This was conclusive evidence that he had not been long in the real estate business and besides his conscientious scruples were in good order. Now if any one can point out a real estate man in modern times who has fallen dead from the same cause I will chip in for a monument to be erected over his grave. When a real estate man of this day and age forgets to hand over a few dollars commission money, he does not drop dead. If he should pay the commission by a mistake, or before he thought, that would be more apt to kill him.

Let us take the case of Judas Iscariot. That man has been disgracefully abused. He went down to his grave in innocence, yet all the world says he was guilty. In his report of the affair, St. Luke said:

"But behold the hand of him that betrayeth me is with me on the table."

"And truly the Son of Man goeth, as it was determined: but woe unto that man by whom he is betrayed."

"And they began to inquire among themselves, which of them it was that should do this thing."

"And there was also a strife among them, which of them should be accounted the greatest."

These words fell upon the ears of the twelve apostles at the Lord's Supper. Now how did Judas Iscariot know that this betraying act would fall upon him? Of course it had to fall upon some one, but that is none of our business. We simply know that Judas got the worst of it.

In a hypnotic state he accepted the thirty pieces of silver from the chief priests and scribes and when he came to his senses and saw what he had done, he went away and got a bale of rope and hung himself. This act alone proves that what he did was done under a psychological influence. While you are pirouetting around on the face of the earth do you ever put yourself in Iscariot's place?

When the stars above are shining we look at them and wonder what they are. When Judas looks down upon us he does not wonder what we are, he knows that we are a lot of roasters.

If the habit of roasting dead ones has grown upon you and you can find no remedy for it, why not pick out some one else. Take Richard III., Nero, Lycurgus and 16 to 1.

Now there was Noah. His name and boat is seldom mentioned except in a jocular way. If you had to do what he did at his age you would say it was no joke.

Think of a boat 450 feet long, 75 feet wide and 45 feet high built by a man 500 years old. He put in one hundred years, one month and seventeen days before he knocked off work and declared the boat finished and ready to float. He did not use any thing but seasoned gopher wood in its construction. I do not know anything about gopher wood but it was certainly all right or else it would never have stood the trip. Think of a pair of every kind of beast, bird, bug, lizard, snake and creeping things, also a lot of extinct animals, that had to be crowded into a space of 450 feet. It took a man like Noah to do that kind of work; a man had to understand his business. There never lived a man who took the liberty of poking fun at Noah who could put all those animals in that boat even if they were cooked, canned, packed and ready for sailors' use. They all had to eat, or die on the trip, for that boat was on the mighty deep for over one year. It certainly took a great pile of feed. Animals like the mastodon and the ichthyosaurus were great eaters. A full grown stud mastodon could eat a ton of hay at one sitting. Noah only had a crew of eight people and they were all old folks. They had to feed and water all these animals you might say in the dark, as there was only one window and they couldn't get much light through that. Noah started on the trip February 17 and landed on Mount Ararat October 1. That is he was stuck there until that time before he could see the top of the mountains. Then it was over four months before he could unload.

It was wonderful what power of endurance Noah had at his age. And after he got back on the earth again he lived three hundred and fifty years. He was a hero. Dewey, Roberts and Schley are not in it with him. This is the reason I say it is unkind to poke fun at him, when he was able to accomplish such a wonderful job, a thing no other man on earth could do.

After the flood Noah took up a homestead, and as soon as his farm dried up, he started to work ploughing and putting in spring wheat. He also started a vineyard which caused him some trouble. If he were alive today we would call it a bad break. The day he got full of grape juice will never be forgotten. There he was in his tent with a B. C. jag on to beat three of a kind. Every time he kicked the quilts off the bed, his sons had to cover him up. It was on this occasion that he got sore on his youngest boy Ham. Moses, in his unpaid writeup of Noah, made no mention of the cause of his death. It is safe to presume, however, that he did not die from grape juice, or he could not have hung onto life nine hundred and fifty years.

It will always be regretted by the people of the earth that Noah set such a bad example. Even unto this day, our young Americans do not believe they can be men un-

less they get blind drunk with the gang and then go home
with a breath that would remove paint.

Lycurgus, or some of those old plutocrats, had the only
liquor cure for drunkards with pride.   Every time a man

HE STARTED TO WORK PLOWING AND PUTTING IN SPRING WHEAT.

collected a vintage and tried to go up two streets at once,
the town marshal took charge of him.   He did not put
him in the lockup, but paraded him around town so
the loafers could give him the horse laugh.   This was

also done to inculcate a lesson in the minds of the children.

That kind of treatment would not work in North Dakota. Just two drinks of that home made tan bark whiskey will put a man past parading. He is seized with fits and goes into a trance and the only way he can be paraded is on a stretcher.

Yes, Noah set a pace that kills. But we must not speak unkindly of him. Let his faults rest with his ashes.

If we could get out of the habit of using grievous words about the dead, and get into the habit of using soft words to the living, there would be less wrath and more sunshine.

If you have an acquaintance or friend who is in hard luck and sore need, do not wait until the poor fellow dies before you open your purse to him. If he could turn over in his grave and see you dumping a lot of roses and violets over his last resting place he would not thank you. He would simply wonder why you did not spend that amount for a porterhouse steak and hot cakes with honey for him, while he was on earth fighting the wolves at his door.

When that certain man went from Jerusalem to Jericho and fell among a lot of sandbaggers and holdup men, they went through him, beat him up and then threw him into a sewer. The Levite and high priest who passed along and saw him half dead never offered to even lift him up and lean his body against a building. In my mind they should have both been pinched. Only for that Samaritan coming along and helping him out of the ditch he perhaps would have perished right there, just for the want of a little help. It will be remembered too that the Samaritan was about broke himself. He only had twopence, but that made no difference. He took the man to a tavern and stood the landlord off for his board, with the promise that if the wounded man's bill amounted to more than twopence he would be traveling that way again and would settle with him.

If that Samaritan was on earth today holding an office with the Chicago Humane Society he would make a great hit.

Cheering words, tenderness, sympathy, the glad mit of good fellowship and a dish of hot beans will brighten and sweeten the life of many a worthy man who is in hard lines.

LEM GRIDLEY.

THE chickens had gone to roost, the song of the red bird had died away, the voices of the ever hungry sand shoats were hushed and the moon was emerging from behind the scraggy hills with her soft beams peeping through the tall sycamores. The stillness of the night was broken only by the cricket's song and the ghost-like notes of a screech owl. While I sat on a bench in front of our house gazing into the cerulean skies and wondering at the immensity of space and why the stars did not bump into each other once in awhile, I heard someone coming up the road whistling. I knew the whistle, and I almost knew the whistler was coming by our place to take me out coon hunting. When he brought up at the gate he said "howdy."

"Is that you, Lem?" I said.

"I reckon yo'ur powerful nigh right. Hits sho' 'nuff Lem Gridley, an' hits th' only name I've ever went by. My dad packed that name 'round clean up to th' time he fit in th' battle uv Pea Ridge; an' thar's whar one o' them Yankee bullets tuck 'im somewhar in the breast, an' we've been decoratin' his grave ever since."

"Well, don't stand there at that gate all night; come in and sit down; this bench is long enough for a dozen slim jims like us. Tell me about your conduct; I have not seen you for a week or two."

"Wall, I run 'bout middlin' in conduct, but my behavior has bin mighty pooh. Yes, sir, I never knowed hit ter run so low ez hit did tuther day. I went ter town an' got inter Andy Washburn's grocery, an' somehow I tuck too much o' that corn dew, an' I went home jist er bilin'. The ole woman an' th' chillun' says I tore down mighty nigh er hundred yards o' worm fence. I reckon they told th' truth ez I've been buildin' fence ever since."

"Well, how are all your folks, Lem?"

"Oh, jist tolerable like, all seem ter be knockin' obout same ez ever. No, I allow I'll have ter take that back; they hain't all so well nuther. You know 'Mandy Stetson is stoppin' at my house since last hog killin' time; she's a kin to the ole woman on her ma's side. Well, she went ter Zeb Patterson's house over at Cross Hollows tuther night ter er shin dig, an' while she wuz dancin' er cow-tillon, th' caller got mixed up. He called out: 'Swing ole Sug,' circle ter th' right, lemonade all an' cage th' bird.' Hit happened ter be 'Mandy's time ter be th' bird an' git caged, an' right whar she wuz dancin' thar wuz er knot hole in th' puncheon, an' I'll be durned ef th' fool gal didn't git one o' her big toes fastened in that hole, an' when she got hit out, thar wuz 'bout forty cents' worth o' toe-hide missin', an' hits 'bout all she kin do ter git er round."

"Have you been coon hunting lately?"

"No, sir, I hain't, an' just 'twixt me an' you, that's what I come by fur tonight ter ax you ef you'd like ter go out fur er spell an' stir up er nest o' coons. Hit's sich er fine night, I allow I couldn't stay ter home."

"All right, Lem, I'll go; but where are your dogs?"

"Hain't got any now, 'cept Towser, an' he's sich er liar, I won't take 'im out. Why, that pesky fool dorg will bark up o' stump."

"Well, what will we do for dogs? I loaned mine to Eli Banks, and he is down on the north fork of the Big Mulberry."

"Tell you what yo' do; yo' jist wait harh 'till I come back. I'll cut er crost th' field thar an' go ove' .er Bill Johnson's an' see ef I kin git his dorgs."

"That's a happy thought. It won't take you more than half an hour to go there and back. I know Bill will loan you his dogs; he would loan a friend his last cup of sugar; and say, Lem, bring his boys along, too; they like a coon hunt as well as anybody."

"Jist leave hit all ter me, I'll soon be back."

Lem Gridley in some ways was a pretty good sort of a fellow. Like all men, of course, he had his faults. He was lanky and round shouldered. He could sit on a fence and watch the weeds choke his corn crop to death and not worry. He was happy all the time, or at least he seemed so. He was a great believer in ghosts and he had no time to put in loafing around grave yards.

If he thought there was no coon hunting in Heaven he would not care to go there. The one room house in which he lived had the appearance of an Arkansaw incubator. He was the father of seven children. Ages respectively one, two, three, four, five, six and seven. Corn "dodgers," blackstrap molasses and middling meat was all that ever graced his table at meal time. He was fond of his liquor, but his circumstances had much to do with keeping him sober. Whenever he went to town he would say to the first person he met:

"'Scuse me fer interruptin' you, but do you know ef thar's ary grocery hyar whar a feller kin git er sweeten' dram?"

The liquor sold there at that time was either apple brandy or corn juice and it would run about 127 proof in the shade. If Lem could swap a coon skin for about three drinks of that moonshine he would let out a yell like a Sioux Indian and start for home. When his children saw him coming they would run under the floor and the cats would climb trees to get out of his way, as it was a known fact that whenever he got drunk he would do some house cleaning, regardless of the season of the year. No man can lay down a rule to follow when he drinks that kind of liquor, for he is liable to denounce his own religion and then steal the corn out of his own crib. It was on these sprees that Lem was sure to see a flock of ghosts, and the way he described them would bring on a chill.

The half hour was up and I heard Lem and the Johnson boys coming across the field.

"Well, I'm back, an' I haint 'lone nuther," Lem said as he halted at the wood pile a few minutes later, with Silas, Bob and Hank Johnson, together with four of the best coon dogs that ever made tracks in Peaceful Valley.

"All right, Lem, I'm ready and I'm glad you brought the boys along. Now where do you think we had better go?"

"Durned ef I know 'less we go over ter 'Possum Hollow; thar ust ter be more coons thar, an' 'round up in th' woods back uv Cliff Morgan's place, than yo' could shake o' stick at. 'Spose we try 'Possum Hollow fust?"

"Yes, that is a regular camping ground for coons. I've hunted there myself," Silas Johnson said.

"Very well, 'Possum Hollow goes," I replied, and we were off.

On one corner of our homestead Lester Perkins had for several years run a cabinet, wagon and carpenter shop. He made coffins for the neighborhood and around his shop could always be seen coffin boxes, some resting on saw-horses and some on the ground. There were also wagon beds, wheels, running gears and the usual piles of hickory and oak timber here and there. A short distance from his shop was a grave yard. It was said to be the most lonesome place in the county. It had furnished many legends for the early settlers. People often wondered how Uncle Lester Perkins could live and work so near that haunted grave yard. The very sight of it at night would make Lem Gridley's teeth chatter. He said it was a regular ghost breeder. I told Lem that it was nearer to 'Possum Hollow by the cabinet shop. He contended that I was wrong. But I coaxed him to go that way, although it was against his wishes.

As we passed by the shop I noticed a covered coffin box on the ground.

On we went until we reached the home of the coons. I may say here that a coon is about one-third the size of a yellow dog. It gives battle best when in water. In time of danger it playfully swims out into deep water and defies all dogs. When it is attacked the dog must understand his business or the coon will drown him.

"Listen! I thought I heard Bowser," Hank Johnson remarked.

"Durned ef you haint right, Hank, that's Bowser's bark, an' he's treed o' coon sho's you're er Swamp Angel," Lem replied.

We all started on the run and soon arrived at the place where Bowser and the rest of the dogs were barking an opening ode up an elm tree.

"Thar hit is! blame my buttons ef hit haint er whopper, too. See 'im out on yon limb, er settin' thar ez sassy ez er crow in watermillion time?" Lem excitedly exclaimed as he stood panting for breath with his head thrown back. The tree was on the bank of a creek and I suspected that we would have some sport. I voluntered to climb the tree and make the coon jump out. Lem gave me a boost and up I went. When I got within seven or eight feet of it the coon made a leap for the water. Bowser plunged in after it and Lem did the coaching after his own style.

"Sic 'em, Bowser!" said he; "that's right! dround 'em, Bowser! git 'em by th' throat an' drag 'em out'n thar! go fur 'em, Bowser!"

Lem was yelling at the top of his voice. Bob and Silas had kept the other dogs back so Bowser had the first round to himself.

"Wonder if Bowser can bring it out alone?" I heard Hank say as I was coming down the tree.

"Bring out nothin'," Lem replied with an uneasy look. "Can't yo' see thar haint near so much splashin'? I'm 'feared Bowser's er gittin' th' wust o' it."

"Gee whiz! we can't lose Bowser! Some of us must go in after him," Silas said with an anxious look.

"You go, Lem," I said.

"Well I should cough up o' cat, 'course I'll go," and in he went.

He waded out but a short distance when he found that Bowser had fought his last coon. He was then into the creek waist deep and still going. He turned to us and said:

"Sic th' dorgs on that blamed coon, fellers, he's makin' fur tuther side."

We did as requested, and it was captured on the other bank by the three dogs. Lem, of course, unmindful of any danger, was going on to the other side to bring back the coon. All at once he stepped into a pot hole and I thought from the time he was under the water he had gone to join Bowser. He finally came up head first blowing and spouting like a porpoise.

"Whee! that durned coon must o' thought I wuz nuther dorg an' tried ter drown' me too," he said, as he scrambled for shallow water.

He waded back to the bank looking like a rat in a rain storm.

"Blame my skin, ef I don't think I'd er drownded ef I'd er stayed under th' water nuther hour longer. I tell you, I had er powerful narrow escape that time. Now some o' yo' fellers go up th' crick 'bout two whoops, er yell an' er whistle from harh, an' you'll find er foot-log; yo' jist cross over ter tuther side an' git that all-fired coon, while I stay harh, an' let some o' that crick water drip off'en me."

"All right, Lem," I said. "Silas and I will bring it over."

We were but a short time bringing back the biggest coon ever caught in 'Possum Hollow.

"Thar's the biggest coon I ever seed, but ez long ez I ever live, an' ez long ez my name is Lem Gridley, I kin never git over er losing that dorg, an' I'm monsters 'feard that Bill Johnson'll be mifted er 'bout us o' losin'

uv 'em. Now bein' ez I'm soaked clean ter th' hide,
I reckon we'd jist ez well be hikin' out fer home."

Hank throwed the coon over his shoulder, we took
a sorrowful look at the place where Bowser had lost his
life and were off for home.

Some little time before we reached the cabinet shop
we came to the forks of a road. I told the boys I was
going to Mr. Wilson's house to borrow his shot gun
for a squirrel hunt next day.

"Better hurry up ef yo' want ter git thar by moonlight, 'caze hits er cloudin' up like Sam Patch, an' I
'spect ter git 'nuther wettin' myse'f 'fore I git home,"
was Lem's remark as I started down the other road.

I had not the least intention of going to Mr. Wilson's. I wanted to reach the cabinet yard ahead of them,
get into that coffin box and play ghost for Lem's benefit.
I did some tall running. My intention was to lie down
in the coffin box and fix the lid over me and when the
boys came along kick it into the air, jump out and give
a scream that would just about frighten Lem to death.
I picked the same box I had noticed as we went out. I
stopped to rest for a moment after my fast run. The
moon was hid behind a black cloud and the wind was
moaning through the elms. Overhead in an oak tree
an owl gave that death-like hoot: "Whoo! whoo!
whoo!" The night was growing darker every minute
from the approaching storm. The heavy thunder seemed
to jar that coffin in front of me. The owls kept on with
their sad wails. The lightning flashed all around and I
was fast giving up the notion of getting into the coffin
box. I thought if I would squat down behind it and
jump up when the boys came by that would do
just as well as getting inside. As I sat down behind
the box I heard some one turn over in it. There was

no use for me to try and believe that I only thought I heard something, for I know that I did. My hair simply lifted my hat straight up. My heart was hammering on my ribs and I was almost transfixed with fright. The storm was growing painfully furious. Those two owls came out on an encore and sang one of their saddest refrains. I could feel my blood turning cold. Just then I heard something breathing in the coffin, a second later it turned over again. The noise could not be mistaken for a myth. I had never believed in ghosts, but I knew there was one in that box. I was afraid to move. I sat there stricken with terror and prayed for the boys to come along. Presently I heard the dogs coming, then I heard the boys talking as they neared the yard. Just as the storm was at its height, the wind was blowing down trees and great limbs were crashing through the timber, the awful noise was indescribable. The boys came along and as they were passing within a few feet of me something terrible took place. I jumped high into the air and screamed. Simultaneously that coffin lid went up and a ghost as white as a sheet jumped out. The awful noise it made was sickening. I heard Lem utter a most pitiful cry and then he started on a dead run, knocking down fences and tearing through the woods like a wild monster. The boys went different directions. I jumped a fence and took across a corn field, breaking down whole rows at a time, and that ghost kept right alongside of me and every time it struck the earth yards of corn stalks were broken down. At last I reached home and fell against the door in a faint, while that ghost leaned against the house breathing heavily. Pa opened the door and found me almost breathless with my hands and face bleeding freely from the cuts made by the corn blades. He pulled me into the house and

the ghost followed.   When I was brought back to life
and got so I could speak all was explained.   The ghost
was a cousin of mine who came to visit us that night
about twenty minutes after I left for the coon hunt.   We

I JUMPED HIGH INTO THE AIR AND SCREAMED.

had both thought of the same trick, only he had gotten
into the coffin.   When I jumped up from behind the
coffin he thought I was a ghost.   When he jumped out
of the coffin I thought he was a ghost, while Lem and

the other boys knew that we were both ghosts. It was some little time before Lem's wounds healed up, as he bumped against trees and fences for nearly five miles. The last time I heard of him was twenty years afterward, and he had not in all that time passed nearer than three miles of that cabinet shop or grave yard.

CHICAGO.

CHICAGO, like every town in the state of Illinois, is more or less situated.

Some of the sidewalks in Chicago are full of knot holes, but they are not wholly objectionable.

The Sun rises and sets in the city limits, i. e.: when the wind does not blow out his light.

Should a young man take his fair one out for a stroll along the scenic banks of the Chicago river; should he become intoxicated with the mellifluent fragrance as it softly oozes adown the gurgling stream, and should gaze into the liquid eyes of his fair one and there and then should he conclude that he couldn't be "hern," and she couldn't be "hisn," he can find good grounds on which to let her slide.

Speaking of the Chicago river: Said river runs eastward as the water gods of Lockport will it. When it flows eastward, it empties into the Chicago Lake. Chicago Lake empties into the Chicago Ocean, and the Chicago Ocean empties into the River of Styx. Passenger boats leave Chicago daily for Charon's Ferry on the tropical Styx; but no return tickets are sold. The wise men of the east do say that emigration to that port is increasing yearly.

Chicago is two feet above the lake level and fifteen miles below Evanston, on the main traveled road to Indiana.

Before Chicago was discovered men of means would often spend thousands of dollars traveling abroad for the purpose of seeing all nationalities. Today that would be sinful extravagance. Any man with the small sum of five cents can take a Milwaukee avenue cable car and see every nationality on earth inside of forty minutes.

Several hundred years ago a cultured old lady of the name of Mother Shipton fell heir to considerable wisdom and forethought. In one of her poems entitled "Future Events," she said: "Iron shall float as easy as a wooden boat." She is right about that. In Chicago iron has been floated, and heavy ore too, that didn't have a trace of iron. All kinds of metal have been floated; just as easy as wood when there was a smart promoter to put the deal through.

The wise old prophetess also said: "In the air men shall be seen in red, blue and green." That also came to pass. If she could have been in Chicago during the panic of 1893 she could have seen men go into the air in more colors than she predicted. It was simply a case of levitation. She also said: "Through hills, men shall ride, with neither horse nor ass at their side." 'That is a cinch. In Chicago they can ride on the hog train, without taking to the hills.

She further said: "Under water men shall talk, sleep and walk." That has almost come true in Chicago. In the street car tunnels under the Chicago river, passengers talk and employees sometimes walk. But there is no sleeping done. The conductors keep everybody awake collecting fares. The only thing that ever gets into Chicago without paying taxes is the light of the moon.

St. Louis is beholden to Chicago for the fine assortment of microbes furnished her, through the drainage canal. Bacteriologists have long been acquainted with the common breed of microbes causing well known contagious diseases. Take for instance consumption; the germ causing that disease is known to medical science as the comma bacillus; comma is the Christian name and bacillus, of course the surname; but why this germ should be called comma is more than I am able to explain. The definition of comma is a short pause in a sentence; a consumptive bacillus has no time to pause—it will not even take an eight-hour shift, but keeps right on doing business until at last it puts the owner of the lungs out of business.

Cerebro spinal meningitis is a contagion caused by the germ diplococus intercellularis, or the gourd-neck bacillus. They run in schools and do a big business wherever they light.

The most spirited, light-footed germ of all is the spirillum choleræ asiaticus. They are the inventors and prime movers in cholera. They demand elbow room and do their rehearsing unmolested. Now comes the Chicago drainage canal germs. They have all the old school microbes skinned to death on up-to-date diseases. St. Louis will stand at the head of the class on microbeology in a few years.

Chicago has some large things standing, such as the Masonic Temple and the city debt.

The saloon keepers in Chicago must be very generous and open hearted, as there are 7,943 of them who hang out signs which read: "Free Lunch Served Here." I never heard of but one man helping himself to a free lunch without paying and he has been a hopeless cripple ever since. No man should try taking saloon lunches without first writing home to his folks and telling them what kind of an epitaph he wants on his grave stone.

The river on the north, Harrison street on the south, the lake on the east and Clinton street on the west surrounds the most congested district in Chicago. When I was a boy I remember the first time I went to town (not Chicago) my folks told me to be careful about crossing the streets, as I might get run over; and if I saw that I was in danger I must run to a telegraph pole and hug it closely. That will not work in Chicago, as teamsters will drive right into a post or telegraph pole just the same as they drive over men, women and children in the streets. No man with a well balanced mind will undertake to cross any street in the above mentioned district without first saying his prayers. Strangers going to Chicago should pay up all back dues on their life insurance policies and get their business affairs in shape so their folks will have no trouble after their death.

When a man starts across Madison street, say, at the Tribune building, he is stopped by a coal wagon going east, and by two express wagons, three buggies, an automobile and a van going west. Somehow he misses them all and advancing a few feet has to turn edgewise to let a brewery wagon pass in front and a garbage wagon behind him. He steps on the car track just in time to back off before a cable car runs over him. Then come six wagons going east and seventeen going west. He is once more on the car track, only to be rung off by the gripman. To save his life he runs west along the track ahead of a team until he gets a chance to turn to the left. Half way down the block he darts between a team and the rear end of a dray, just in time to run into a coal wagon. After that passes, he is chased back east to the corner of the Hartford building and by a quick dash between two other teams he reaches the sidewalk. If he is not crippled he will have a sinful soul, because he swore enough at the teamsters to break up the whole plan of salvation.

If a man can make his way to an elevated station he stands some chance of living. I knew a farmer who went to Chicago to visit his married daughter. She lived on Sixty-third street and he was instructed by letter when he arrived at the North-Western depot at 8:30 a. m. to go to the elevated station at Clark and Lake streets. This he did, but in place of taking a South Side train he went to Logan Square. When he returned he thought perhaps he had taken the train at the wrong station, so he climbed the stairs at State and Lake streets. This time he went to Douglas Park. He tried another station and went to West Fortieth avenue. By this time it was night, so he put up at a hotel on Clark street and the next morning hired an express wagon to take him to Sixty-third street. The most serious thing about this joke is that old residenters often take the wrong entrance at stations and pay fare twice.

The only way to be safe in Chicago is to buy a ticket on some railroad and leave town.

Chicago is a poor place for a man if he is broke, unless he is sure he can borrow money from a lamp post.

Chicago is a great place to introduce a stranger out of his money. When I say introduce I mean that he will meet a friend nine times out of ten somewhere. He invites the friend to join him in a smile. They go into Jim's or Jack's place and there the friend will meet nine old college chums—all thirsty—and at once the friend introduces the stranger to the sloppy nine, or as the friend

calls them, the bunch or the push.   Then all the stranger
can say, is:

"Gentlemen, we were just going to have something;
won't you join us?"

THERE THE FRIEND RUNS INTO TWENTY-THREE MEMBERS OF THE
HOTFOOT CLUB, OF WHICH HE IS THE PRESIDENT.

"Oh—we don't mind," is the answer in concert.

They all call for fifteen cent drinks, because the
stranger looks like ready money.   So in that place the
stranger is introduced out of $1.65.   Then the friend and
the stranger try another place.   There the friend runs

into twenty-three members of the Hotfoot Club, of which he is the president. The stranger is promptly introduced to that bunch and of course invites them to have something. No member has the nerve to refuse.

"How much, please?" says the stranger to the Frumenti prestidigitator.

"$3.75," is the polite answer from the man in white.

It is then 9:30 a. m., only two places have been visited, yet the stranger has been introduced out of $5.40.

Chicago is a great place for people to grow downhearted and despondent. The sunshine of life fades away. They are heavy of heart and every hope slowly sinks into obscurity. There is an old saying: "It is always darkest before dawn." I heard a Chicago man once say, that if it got much darker with him he would have to get a lantern.

A few years ago I attended the "Twelve Temptations" at the Chicago opera house. After the play I went to the North Side to meet a friend. Passing through Washington Place I noticed a woman sitting on one of the park seats with her face buried in her hands. I wondered if she could be waiting for a car in the middle of the park. As I neared my destination I could not dismiss the woman and her seeming distress from my mind. I could not persuade myself to think otherwise than that she was in deep trouble. I halted at the north end of the park, looked back, and could see a dim form. She had not moved. I have always tried to be a philanthropist and have a warm spot in my heart for anyone in distress. I resolved that I would return and see if I could in any way assist that broken-hearted woman. I turned back and when I came up to her I said: "You will pardon me, miss, for addressing you, but seeing you here in the park on a cold winter night like this I was led to believe you were in trouble and if you want any assistance I will do all in my power to aid you." She looked up at me with piercing eyes and said:

"Say, young feller, now don't you get gay, or I'll call a cop and have you pinched, see?"

I said no more and walked away with a misogynist's tread. I had reached the conclusion that she was not the thirteenth temptation.

It is not every one who finds gloom and grief in Chicago—some of them take it with them.

One day while roaming around in Lincoln park I came across a man resting his elbows on the back of a seat trying to wail away his life.

I asked him what he was crying about. He looked up for an instant and then buried his face in his hands deep enough to hide his cow-lick and said:

"My story is a sad one. When a boy, less than fifteen years old, I joined the army. I wanted to do something to make my name famous and give history a chance to fill up on some new stuff. I did not do much fighting, as the company to which I belonged was not out for that purpose. We had many fields of action and did great work in our way. Our captain was a log thief in Wisconsin before the war. As well as I remember we were about 300 strong, armed to the teeth.

"The most crushing time in my war experience was when we had charge of a boat traveling up White river in Arkansaw. The object of our trip was to make a collection of supplies and do a general pilfering business in the interest of our captain, who always kept the change. I distinctly remember the first stop we made. A large, white house on the river bank looked deserted and lonesome. The captain ordered us to take everything in sight. We transferred to our boat 600 pounds of hams, two bar-

rels of salt and many other things. The men connected
with the farm had gone to fight for their country, leaving the women and one or two aged wing-footed coons.
Ah! to this day I can see that poor woman as she stood
upon the door steps with her two daughters, crying and
pleading with us brave soldiers not to take everything.
She said they had no way to earn a living and starva-
tion would surely come to them. Our captain cared
not for their tears and ordered us to leave nothing behind but our record, and that record is today painted
upon my brain in dull smoke color and it is killing me
by inches.

"Day after day we traveled up that river, stopping at
every house where we thought we could make a haul.
Many times I tried to make my escape from the boat
but could not and had to stay and take the regular dose.
When the war ended I began to reflect and suffer with
remorse. As time passed I grieved harder and louder
and more of it. I saw plainly that I could not live
long if I did not get my wailing checked. I took pills
and pellets and all the drugs I could get but without
effect. At last I decided to come to Chicago, as I had
been told that the noise and lake winds would assist me
in departing from this life. I find this to be true, and
now feel that the end is near."

I asked him on what side he belonged during the
war. He said he did not remember, but rather thought
he did not belong to either side, as the people called him
and his company jayhawkers.

I tried to console him by singing a little song filled
with pathos and sentiment. His eyes were blinded with
scalding tears and before I had finished the first stanza
he had fallen to the ground in a globular heap. I assisted

him a to comfortable seat under an oak and asked him
if I could help him.

"No, sir," he said, in a low feeble voice, "except I
wish you wouldn't sing."

I TRIED TO CONSOLE HIM BY SINGING A LITTLE SONG FILLED WITH
PATHOS AND SENTIMENT.

Chicago is well supplied with matrimonial agencies.
If a man is at all anxious to get married he can soon
be a husband, breathing upon the front tooth of a loving wife.

I received the following letter from the Chicago Gordian Knot Matrimonial Agency a short time ago:

"Dear Sir: We take the liberty of enclosing a few specimen descriptive photos (selected at random) of ladies who belong to the Gordian Knot Private Agency. These ladies all desire gentlemen either with a view to matrimony or for amusement. If none of these suit you we have hundreds of others to select from. Remit us $2 and give us a transparent idea of the kind of ladies with whom you wish to correspond. We have lady members of every age and color; black, white or tan; any religion or nationality; living in every part of the United States. We introduce each gentleman to fifteen ladies. Out of that number he ought to be able to choose a congenial correspondent. All questions cheerfully answered. If you have any doubt about our being able to please you write us and we will state distinctly what we can do for you. When your case and $2 in money is placed in our hands it will receive our personal attention, and all your wants will be carefully considered. Our business is confidential. You will notice photo No. 3,602, Tyrone, Anderson county, Ky. She is a grass widow, chuck full of fun, very affectionate and in business for herself. She desires the companionship and coddling of a good husband. She is forty-three past; stands ten hands and four inches high barefooted. Has means and will inherit more. She would not care for a husband whose breath could be ignited with a match, or one who combs his hair with a towel.

"No. 3,527, St. Paul, Decatur county, Ind., is a beauty. Has a little money—to get—and is healthy; is affectionate and seldom chews gum. Weighs 110 pounds in summer, but fattens up some during the winter. She toes in a little, but none to hurt. She has roan hair; is

"SHE IS A GRASS WIDOW, CHUCK FULL OF FUN, VERY AFFECTION-
ATE AND IN BUSINESS FOR HERSELF."

a little shy and pouty at times. You would like her. Her first three husbands are dead.

"No. 438 is a perfect dream. Her long eyelashes are enough to torment a man in his grave. She is buxom, frisky and kittenish. She is from good stock and is itching to get married. We think you would not be taking any chances—even though you may think that marriage is a failure—in buckling onto this girl, for she is the finest looker that ever trotted in a shirt waist.

"In our list you will find several hundred members ranging in age from 16 to 73. Knowing our ability to please we would like to hear from you."

I am forced to believe that the Gordian Knot Wedlock Bureau was a little overpresumptuous in my case. In the first place I am not on the market. Again I think their charges are too high; $2 is too much for a wife, where you are only allowed a choice of fifteen women. Had they looked up my standing in Dun's or Bradstreets' agencies they could have seen that I am a man who would not care to tie up to a woman selected at random. In my mind marriage is a failure, unless the husband has plenty of fortitude and groceries, accompanied by compatibility of temperament and a cash income. Otherwise—otherwise.

Chicago some years has two seasons, July and winter.

Chicago has the most accommodating department stores in the world. In passing through them one sees hundreds of signs and cards reading:

"Special price on hard and soft coal, gas stoves, laundry soap and alarm clocks today."

"We do horseshoeing and wagon tire setting at half price."

"Moles, warts and superfluous hair removed on the fifth floor. Take the elevator."

"WEIGHS 110 POUNDS IN SUMMER, BUT FATTENS UP SOME DURING THE WINTER."

"Coal oil, hair vigor, kindling wood and fly paper reduced 33 1-3 per cent."

"Pet monkeys, Peruvian tom cats, tigers, elephants and salt codfish on the top floor, sold at less than cost."

"Dentistry on second floor. Have your teeth plugged with zinc, very cheap."

"New spring styles of burial caskets now on sale."

"Plough harness, cheese, lime, ice cream and shirt waists in the basement."

"Try our restaurant on the fourth floor. Coffee and doughnuts five cents."

"Hair oil, fountain pens, pine tar, smokers' articles and Spanish lace reduced as advertised."

"Leave your measure for a new set of teeth today, $1.69."

"We have just received a large bankrupt stock of fine cigars, which are now on sale. All of the twenty-five-cent brands will be sold at three for five cents."

"Our farm implement department is complete. Separators, binders, drag harrows, sod ploughs, rakes, mowers, corn planters and fan mills always sold at cost."

"Today special cut price on gas fixtures, ladies' hose, lead pipe, standard corsets, picture frames, buggy robes, cathartic pills, matches, foulard silks and axle grease."

"Great reduction in mixed candy, unlaundried shirts, New Orleans molasses, shoe polish, horse liniment, sewing machine oil and suspenders during this great sale."

"Barber shop on third floor. Hair cut, shave and shine reduced to 19 cents."

"Corns, bunions, ingrowing toe nails, chilblains and enlargement of the feet successfully treated at half price on the second floor."

"Veterinary surgeon, phrenologist and clairvoyant in the bicycle department."

"Try our fifteen-year-old rye whiskey.   Reduced from $1.50 per quart to 29 cents."

"Photographs taken at one-third the regular price to-day."

"SHE IS THE FINEST LOOKER THAT EVER TROTTED IN A SHIRT WAIST."

"A great bargain in all-wool pants, maple syrup, pocket knives, fast colored socks, tar roofing, tinware, rat poison and perfumes."

"Cord wood, sheet music, lampblack, toilet soap, varnish and sweet pickles always on hand."

"A sweeping reduction on pianos, turpentine, cigarettes, fresh eggs, lace curtains, mining machinery and early garden stuff today."

"See our special offer on razor strops, steam boilers, padlocks, dandruff cure, smokeless powder and family **Bibles.**"

"Blacksmithing and hand laundry in the basement."

"Manicuring and Turkish baths on third floor."

The fact is a person can find almost anything in a big department store except a football game and a Methodist revival.

Chicago is a great place for people to fall into habits; some of which are serious and oft times fatal. Take for instance the deadly doughnut. A man who falls a victim of the doughnut habit is a hopeless wreck. There is no cure, no help or relief for him. His star of hope has twinkled for the last time. The glory of the day is but a flash of sadness. The balmy eves of life are dark dreary caves, where the flapping of bats' wings echo down through the ghostly corridors, into eternity.

A doughnut is a small hole entirely surrounded with bullet proof dough, and day after day in Chicago it claims new victims. What an awful thing to contemplate when you see a strong, healthy young man falling into that habit. It is but a short time until the doughnut symptoms show in his face. It takes on the hue of old tallow, and his eyes resemble a pair of fried eggs. He soon loses his elastic step and goes dragging his feet like a renegade steer calf after the breaking up of a hard winter in the northern part of Manitoba. He soon becomes emaciated and cadaverous looking. He is no longer garrulous, no longer that nimble, bright, sunny-natured

IT IS BUT A SHORT TIME UNTIL THE DOUGHNUT SYMPTOMS SHOW
IN HIS FACE.

mother's joy that he once was. Instead he is a wretched piece of humanity wandering around waiting for Father Time to cut him down in the lexicon of youth, that no more rememberance might be had of such a degenerate as he.

As a commercial city, Chicago has no equal, but a great deal of the business is done on a psychological basis. Chicago people are hospitable, whole souled and generous; a stranger visiting there, however, would do well to take his lunch with him, in case of an accident.

Chicago is a great place, for a man to place himself, if that place is the place where he wants to be placed.

LEXICON OF SLANG.

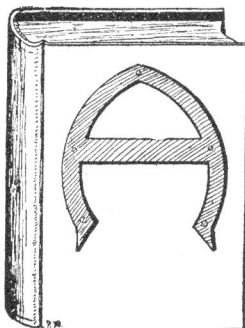

NGEL, *n.* a lobster with money.

America, *n.* a dump for the Chinese Empire.

Brain-Spavin, *n. a.* a case of swell head; enlargement of the cocoa.

Bazoo, *n.* an augean mouth.

Bone-orchard, *a. n.* the last resting place; over the river; a grave-yard.

Booze-fighter, *a.* one who enters into a contest for supremacy fighting the red stuff and never wins out.

Copper, *n.* a club swinger; a somnambulist.

Cinch, *adv.* holding a job in a bank.

Cheese, *n.* the proper caper; getting money from home.

Cigarette, *n.* an undertaker's companion; pipe-sticks; a weapon of Father Time.

Drag, *adv.* influence; marrying a widow with a large wad of dough.

Dub, *n.* one who hasn't sufficient backbone to be a fool.

Duffer, *n.* a wart; a protuberance; a thing; a parody on mankind.

Easy street, *adv. n.* a street on which few people ever travel.

Eli, *p. n.* one who gets there; one who is full of ambition and prunes.

Elysium, *n.* a happy home for the virtuous after death, although no one on this ball of dirt has ever heard from there.

Football, *n.* a barbarous game played by a wild tribe in North America; a game in which many are kicked to death.

Fleece, *v.* to take belongings from another without being introduced.

Frozen-face, *n.* a face shown to those who are shy on funds; a face easy to find, but never looked for.

Flim-flam, *v.* to separate people from their earnings while they are looking on.

Freeze-up, *v.* to turn to a cake of ice when invited to loosen up.

Gall, *n.* a redundancy of unparalleled temerity.

Galoot, *n.* see dub.

Growler, *n.* a can of suds.

Glad-hand, *n.* a generous mit extended in olden times, now obsolete.

Hand-out, *adv.* a feed for the children of the blind baggage.

Hog-train, *n.* a train always filled and run entirely by the passengers.

Hammer, *v.* a tool used by a knocker, often doing great damage.

Hand-me-down, *adj.* a ready made suit of clothing reduced from $18.39 to $3.98.

Hot-air, *v.* fruitless guff; an erroneous application of wind, usually given by one who has no mental power or influence.

It, *n.* the whole thing; one who can borrow money.

Ice-man, *n.* one whose praises have been sung throughout the land with a loud voice, but it was all a joke.

Jolly, *v.* guff that is often given as part payment of an old bill.

Josh, *v.* a man who has discovered that he was put on this earth for no purpose.

Jag, *n.* temporary derangement of the nut.

Kalamazoo, *n.* a theatrical joke.

Lobster, *n.* see Slob.

Lid, *n.* a sky piece; a covering for the nut.

Lilacs, *n.* strings; gallways; spikes; oakum; whis-kers; spinach; ribbons.

Mit, *n.* bread-hook; lunch-lifter.

Mud, *n.* a common name for common people.

Nut, *n.* a think-tank; a shell where schemes are pre-concerted.

Nutty, *adv.* going wrong; daffy.

Nonsense, *adv.* nine-tenths of modern conversation, the balance is mostly profanity.

Nourishment, *adv.* formerly bread, now booze and to-bacco.

No-place, *n.* a land where wealth has no influence, and people are valued on their merits.

Oyster, *n.* one who hopes the world will madly rush on while he sleeps.

Printer, *n.* a galley slave.

Pipe, *n.* aberration of the head; to drift from the truth unconsciously; dreaming with open eyes.

Pippin, *n.* see peach.

Peach, *n.* a fairy with the beauty of Psyche and the sweetness of Aurora.

Pinched, *v.* see pulled.

Pulled, *v.* one who rides in a wagon at the expense of the municipality.

Quits, *adv.* a common occurrence with a summer engagement; a divorce.

Rabbit, *n.* a guy with short weight gray matter.

Rag, *n.* a publication in which the affairs of a nation are satisfactorily settled.

Rush-act, *adj.* a system worked by one who is looking for easy money.

Soak, *v.* to successfully deliver an upper cut; a blow above or below the belt.

Skinned, *v.* one who has been bunkoed, touched, held up and sent home hungry.

Skate, *n.* a slob; a bum gazabo.

Squeeze, *n.* a past grand master of the bunch.

Sinker, *n.* a fried wad of wheat dough, used to alleviate a rodent sensation in the pyloric orifice.

Sore, *adj.* a person who is invited to take a drink, and then has to settle for it.

Touched, *v.* a man who has been relieved of his room rent.

Tramp, *n.* one who would drop dead at the sight of a cord of wood.

Uncle, *n.* a keeper of diamonds, watches and overcoats, just to be accommodating.

Vexed, *v.* trying to cash a check among strangers.

Water-wagon, *n.* a vehicle used by people who cut out the booze spasmodically.

LEAVING THE FARM.

IT always kind of hurts me when I think of how boys on a farm are treated. Many of them do not have the chance of a tramp cat. It is a case of work year in and year out, and never rest. No wonder they pack their duds into a grain sack once in awhile and leave home. The eternal monotony drives them to it. It is my earnest belief that a farmer does not know how to keep his boys at home.

Take the case of the Prodigal Son. He got tired of the farm and asked his father to give him his portion of truck and turn over, as he intended to pack up and skip out. His father did as he was requested. It was not long before the Prodigal was journeying toward a town where he could spend his savings. He evidently got into a pretty swift town, as he lived like a riotous prince as long as his coin lasted.

Of course something had to happen so he could tell a hard luck story. As soon as he went broke, a famine set in and he had to carry the banner and go without his coffee and rolls. If there is anything on earth that will make a young farmer sad it is sleeping in a park, washing his face in the river and postponing his breakfast. It is then he recalls the good things he had at home; such as hot soda biscuits, sweet butter, ham gravy and coffee that his Ma used to make.

The Prodigal did not know what to do. He was a stranger in a strange land. He had neither trade nor profession. He was a farmer plain and simple, broke and hungry. On his own recommendation he got a job of a citizen feeding hogs. That kind of work in those days was by no means pleasant, besides it in a way stigmatized a fellow's raising. He soon grew tired of the job and could think of nothing but home and how nice it would be to get back. He felt he would be willing to do any old thing around home just for his board and clothing. He made up his mind he would act as one of the hired men and be willing to wait for the second table when his folks had company, if he could enjoy the blessings of home once more. He was willing to make any sacrifice just to be back by the old fireside where he could rest his feet on the mantelpiece as he had done in other days.

He thought it all over and made up his mind to go home and tell his Pa everything and make him a promise to be a better boy if he would take him back. He would even sleep in the smokehouse and eat with the servants.

He announced to the ancient plebeian that he could feed his own hogs, as he was going home and he wanted to get there in time to help out with the haying. He did not have a definite idea of the kind of a reception he would get when he reached home, but he had made up his mind to take chances and get away from that drove of hogs.

When he was within a few hundred yards of his home his father saw him coming through the rye, and went out to meet him and give him a hearty welcome. The old man fell upon his neck and was exceedingly glad of his return. He told the servants to bring out the best all-wool robe on the place, put some Sunday shoes on his feet and a forty karat opal ring on his hand. Then he ordered a corn-fed calf butchered and commanded a haste of the feast. After the banquet there was music and a social hop which contributed much to the merriment, and everyone was glad.

Just about this time the elder son came in from the field where he had been working. He heard a racket in the house and asked one of the servants what it was all about. The servant told him his long lost brother had returned and that his father was giving him a blowout. The elder brother did not like this and refused to go into the house, although his father came out and labored with him. He was sore, however, and informed his father that he had served him for many years and had at no time transgressed one of his commandments, and in all that time he had never received even so much as a kid that he might have a banquet and make merry with his friends. His brother, however, had been away spending his earnings like a sailor and living like a king, and on his return the finest Durham calf in the fleet had been killed and a feast given him, while a smoker and dance concluded the program. Can you blame the elder son for getting sore?

The story of the Prodigal Son should be a lesson to every farmer. It is not human nature for a farmer's son to stay at home working day in and day out, ploughing corn, building fences and clearing land without some amusement now and then to break the monotony. He is different from a slab of basswood in that he has feeling. He yearns to skip the mazy glazy glide now and then. He wants a touch of high life. He looks about him when the summer is ended and the grain is garnered. He thinks of the long winter before him with no amusement in store. It's the same old story: eat, work and sleep. Suppose a young man should walk up to his farmer father and say:

"See here, Pa, I am a grown man now. I have worked assiduously for you for many years. I have been a faithful dog from start to finish. I have been a slave for you in all kinds of weather. I have sawed wood in the daytime and husked corn at night, and now I want you to get up a little party for me. Invite some of the neighbors and give me a swell time. What say you?"

"A swell time, eh! You are a pretty looking stripling to come to me with such nonsense. You go on and finish cutting that patch of corn stalks, or I'll get a hickory club and tan your jacket, you tow-headed scamp, you."

When a boy gets that kind of an answer, he has to go out behind the ash hopper or some place where he can be alone for a while until that fit of anger passes away. If he didn't do this he is liable to call his father an old hayseed, and then there would be a family misunderstanding.

A farmer should talk to his boys more, and use the pick-handle less. He should make it a point to turn his corn-crib into an athletic room every winter and give his boys a few lessons on the manly art of self-defense and other sports along that line. He should teach them tencent limit and how to deal from the bottom so that when they go to town, if they should fall into a quiet game they would not be so easy to skin. He should have a homemade pool table in his woodshed for rainy days. He should deliver a course of lectures on occultism, theosophy, the science of necromancy, or talks on ornithology and zoology so they can distinguish a buzzard from a jack rabbit. He should give them a theoretical knowledge of how to plough without sweating. He should teach them to read well, beginning on something easy, like Milton's Paradise Lost, Dante's Inferno and Deuteronomy. A few hints on astrology and stud poker and a knowledge of centrifugal and centripetal forces might be

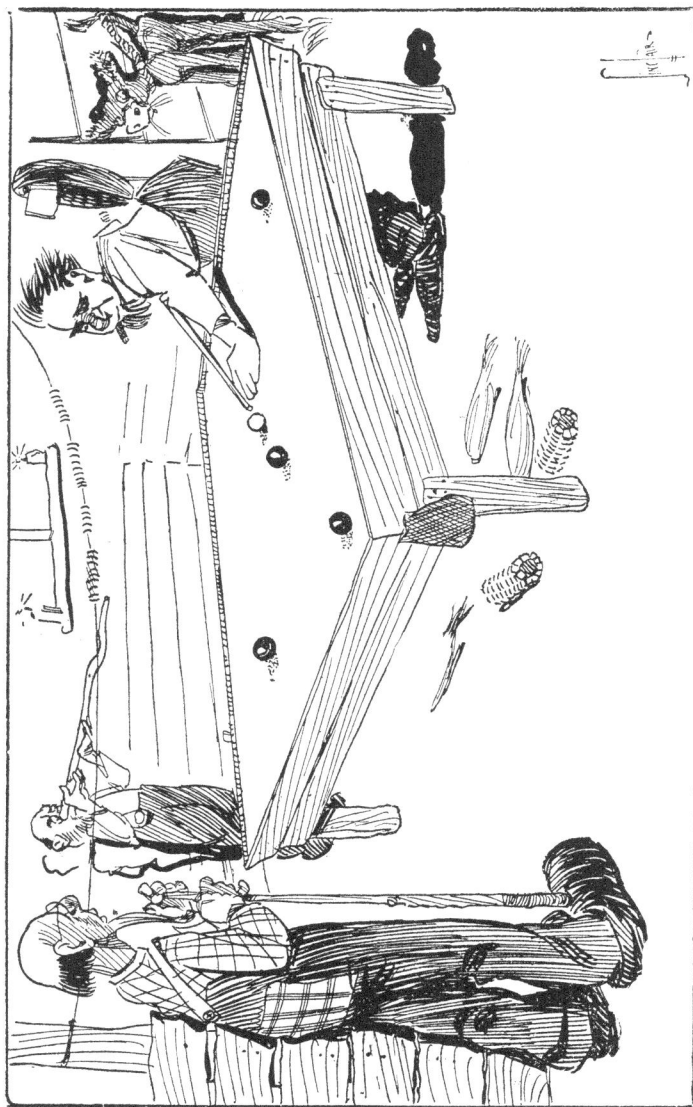

HE SHOULD HAVE A HOME-MADE POOL TABLE IN HIS WOODSHED FOR RAINY DAYS

beneficial. He should teach them to play the piano and seven up. He should give them an idea of the intrinsic and extrinsic value of life; they should be well up on physiognomy, mental telepathy, parliamentary law, ethnography and table etiquette. There is nothing quite so embarrassing as to see a farm boy feeding himself with squash pie by means of a knife. Now all this can be done with but little trouble and the farmer can bring his boys out of the kinks and make them presentable to the city folks. Besides, they would have no desire to run away from home, as home would be made happy for them, and they would also be up to date.

I grew tired of the farm at one time just because I did not think that I was properly entertained. I wanted to play Prodigal Son, so I could return home some day and have a reception. I was hungry for a change. I wanted music and song. I wanted to get into the mad whirl and go around a few times. I wanted to see an elephant walk a rope. I wanted to see strange faces, and forever get away from the song of the scythe on the grindstone. I was tired of the hoe, and was willing to go Prodigally wrong just to try it.

The day I had set aside for leaving came and I started. I did not know where I was going, I just knew that I was leaving the farm, that was all. I gave a farewell glance at the milk-pans on a bench in front of the house. The dogs wanted to follow me, but I drove them back. The old well-sweep and the curling smoke from the chimney were the last things in view. A robin red-breast lighted on the fence by the roadside and sang a few notes as I traveled on over the flint rocks in the direction of the Indian Nation.

Night overtook me and I found a resting-place in a hollow tree. My sleep was by no means peaceful, as some varmints claimed the tree and they felt put out when they found it occupied. They set up a dreadful howl and kept it up until daybreak. I was glad to see that time come, as I was hungry and cramped. I climbed the tree, made a breakfast of wild grapes, and then I moved on toward the west. In the afternoon I came to a negro cabin and heard someone playing a banjo. I met an old black mammy at the door and asked her for some buttermilk and corn pone.

"Lawdy, lawdy, honey, 'course yo' kin jist git yo' fill right heah; you'se er lookin' powerful hongry Ize er tellin' you. Sot yosef on dis heah nail kag 'n I brung yo' somethin' ter tuck eraway dot darh pain from under yo' vest. Yo' looks mighty like er boy leavin' home. I done seed so many uv 'em, I jist knows eber time I sees 'em. Now, harh yo' is, honey; eat dis harh bread 'n milk, 'n yo' sho' to feel jist like a shoat in er co'n-field in no time."

I certainly did enjoy that meal and the plink and plunk and plunk and plink of that banjo in the hands of an old negro in one corner of the cabin. I thanked them both and started on my journey. I had gone but a short distance when I heard the clatter of horses' feet. For some reason a cold chill crept up my back and I was fearful of some impending danger. I was afraid to look back. I felt that someone was after me, and I was right, too, for just then Pa and three neighbors galloped up from behind. Pa did not ask me many questions. He ordered me to get up behind him, which I did, and we started in the direction of home. We reached there late at night, and when Pa had stabled his horse and the neighbors had gone on their way, he invited me into the peach orchard. He was very active that night; in fact, I never remember of having seen him so busy. Before he started in on me he said:

HE USED UP PEACH TREE SPROUTS RIGHT AND LEFT.

"It pains me, my son, to be compelled to thrash you, for it hurts me more than it does you."

Now this expression was not original with Pa; others have used it. For all that, I can not see how to figure it out. I must be very obtuse, for if that licking hurt him more than it did me, he would have thought seriously of asking the governor to call out the state militia. He used up peach tree sprouts right and left. I think he got the idea out of the Bible, where it reads: "Spare the rod and spoil the child." It seemed to me that on that occasion he was dead bent on spoiling the child.

I had missed my guess a long way. He did not meet me out in the rye field and fall on my neck with unbounded joy. He did not put store-boughten shoes on my feet and a ring on my finger. It is true, he fell on my neck in that orchard, but not after the manner I had expected.

Although this happened when I was quite a small boy, I am to this day more or less nervous when I walk through a peach orchard.

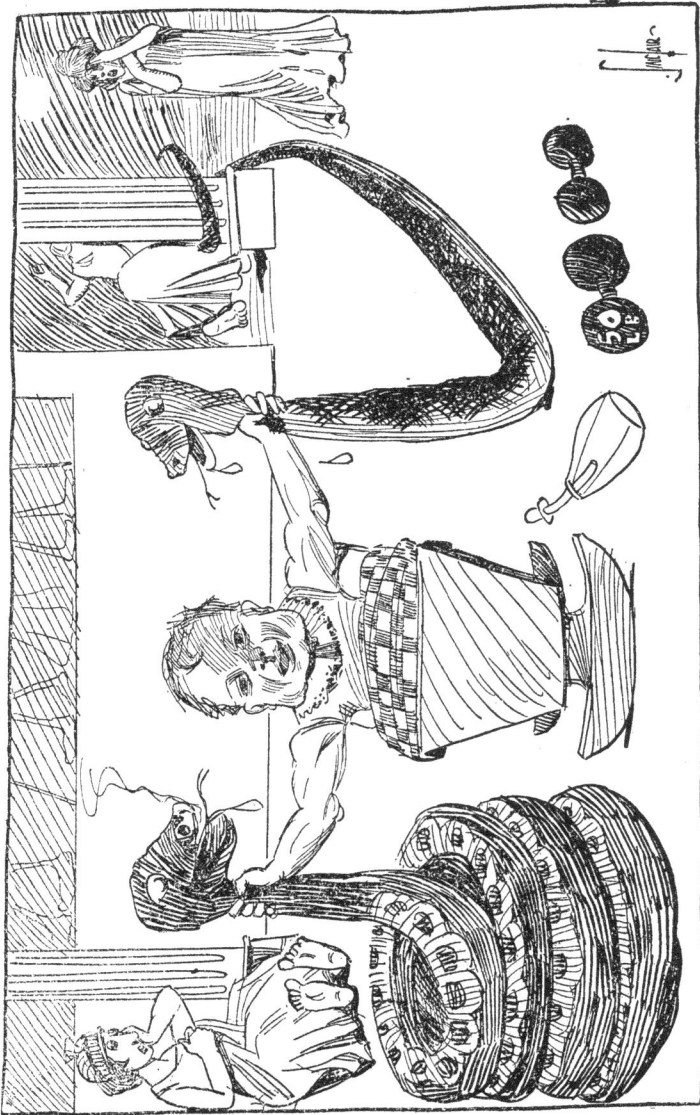

HE JUST TOOK THE SNAKES BY THEIR THROATS—ONE IN EACH HAND—AND CHOKED THEM TO DEATH.

HERCULES.

HAVE always thought it a fortunate thing for Hercules that he was precocious (whatever that means), as Juno was hostile to him from the time he was spawned. Every time she even thought of him she would put on a fresh coat of war paint and her hair would turn green. She used to sit up at night scheming how she could give him the worst of it. While Hercules was teething she managed to put a pair of ugly-looking snakes in his cradle, with the idea that they would put an end to him, but they didn't. When he awoke and discovered the snakes, he braced himself, told the servants to stand aside and they would see a scrap that would make a Roman gladiator look like thirty cents. He never had any time for upper cuts or fancy jabs. He just took the snakes by their throats—one in each hand—and choked them to death.

This made Juno feel small, and just for spite she, with her high grade hypnotic monkey business rendered Hercules a subject to one of his relatives whose name was Eurystheus. This relative forced upon Hercules a number of dangerous and bold adventures, all of which seemed impossible. The first thing this Mr. Eurystheus ordered him to play dog, go into the valley of Nemea and chase up

CITY BILL POSTING
COMING!
NEXT WEEK AT THE COLOSSEUM
HERCULES, THE STRONG BOY
VS.
THE TERRIBLE GREEK.
GRAECO-ROMAN

HE THEN RESORTED TO HIS FAVORITE SPORT—THE CHOKING ACT—AND THAT SETTLED IT.

a certain lion that had for a long time been a terror to the natives. He was to skin him and bring in his hide. Hercules found the lion and tried to kill him with a four-year-old club, but failed. He then resorted to his favorite sport—the choking act—and that settled it. He threw the dead lion over his shoulder and took it into town. When Eurystheus saw what Hercules had done he requested a friend to hold his coat while he fainted. Fainting, it will be remembered, was in those days a fad. When he had recovered he said to Hercules:

"Now you go out on the edge of town to tell about your lion fight. If you should tell it in the city limits it is liable to cause a panic."

He was all worked up over the hero's prodigious strength, and the news soon spread far and wide about the new heavyweight.

His next job was to slaughter the Hydra. I do not know what we would call a Hydra, if such a beast lived in this age. A pipe dream, I guess, would be it's nickname. It had nine angry heads which it tossed with fretful spleen. The middle head was immortal, and that was the head which kept Hercules guessing. The Hydra hung out in a swamp near Argos, and it was certainly a hard proposition. Hercules found it resting in its nest. He started in to make a few passes with his club. The first pass he made, off went a head, but to his great surprise, two new ones grew forth. Then he clubbed off another head, and two more new ones grew out in the same place. Then he told his under dog Iolaus to heat some irons and he would try burning off the heads because they were growing on too thick for him. This plan was successful with all except the immortal head. He had to cut that off and put it under a big forty-ton rock.

IT HAD NINE ANGRY HEADS WHICH IT TOSSED WITH FRETFUL SPLEEN.

196

History makes no mention of the Hydra's body. It may have been that the varmint had no body, just a lot of hideous heads sticking up to frighten people to death.

It seems that Hercules' work got harder all the while. Just as soon as he got through beating the heads off that Hydra, he had to go to a cattle man by the name of Augeas and dung out his stable. It turns out that this man Augeas was a very shiftless kind of a fellow, although he was King of Elis. That doesn't count, however, there are plenty of shiftless kings. He owned a lot of cow-sheds which he called the Augean stables and for thirty years or so he had kept a herd of 3,000 steers there without the place having been cleaned. Most of these steers were too stiff to walk. They were stocked and bunged up with hoof-rot and scratches. Hercules looked the ground over for a few moments and a happy thought struck him. The Alpheus and Peneus rivers were handy and he turned both streams into the stables and sluiced them out in one day. It is too bad that that kind of work is a lost art. It would be a great thing to improve the sanitary condition of some of the modern cities of America.

The next task Hercules had was an easy one. Eurystheus had a daughter he called Admenta, and woman-like she was always looking for something to wear different from that of other women. There was a war-like nation of females known as Amazons. The queen of these hens bore the name of Hyppolyta (from her name she must have been amphibious). She owned a girdle which was perhaps cut on the bias and strictly up to date, and as Admenta had heard about it, she told her Pa that she must have it. Eurystheus told Hercules to fix himself out with a boat and a company of brave men and go after the girdle. After a hard trip and many narrow escapes he reached the land of the Amazons. Right here I will say I have lost all respect for Hercules. He is no friend of mine, as I have no time for a man who will strike a woman.

Hyppolyta received Hercules kindly, and said she would give up the girdle without trouble. At this point Juno got in with her hammer (a tool she never dropped except at meal times). She took the form of an Amazon and went all over the country telling the other Amazons that Hercules and his gang were carrying off their queen. So they instantly arrayed themselves and went down to Hercules' ship about 200,000 strong. Hercules thought perhaps the queen was acting in bad faith, and the result was sad. He was seized with that habit of choking people and the Amazon queen was taken back to her wigwam a corpse. Hercules then took the girdle and sailed for home. I suppose he felt jolly and in high spirits after choking the breath out of that poor old woman and taking from her a girdle that probably wasn't worth more than $6.98 wholesale.

As soon as he returned home he had to start right out again. This time it was a very hard proposition. Eurystheus wanted Hercules to bring him the ox Geryon, a big brute with three bodies. He had been seen on the Island of Erytheia. (This perhaps was the land of Spain, that is, if Spain was an island at that time.) After tramping over many kingdoms, Hercules reached Libya and Europe. I do not know how he could land in two countries at the same time, but he did. Now here is where he certainly got strong. He raised the two mountains of Calpe and Abyla. He did this simply to keep in practice and leave a mark of progress. Some historian who wrote as though he had been introduced to Hercules, said that he (Hercules) rent one mountain into two and left half on each side forming a strait now called Gibraltar. When you sail through that passage you can observe on both sides the Pillars of Hercules. Other writers have gone so far as to dispute this statement, and have plainly said that they did not believe one-half of it.

But to return to the big steer of Geryon. He was guarded by a giant named Eurytion, and a two-headed bulldog. They did not bluff Hercules. He spat on his hands and went at them, and once more laid the foundation for a comedy drama, entitled "Choked to Death." Then he surrounded the Geryon steer and took him away to Eurystheus. History says he picked up other steers along the road and took them in also.

Hercules grew so popular with his boss that he kept him on the road all the time. He proved to be the most successful traveling man in mythological times. Only he worked on a different basis from traveling men of today. A modern traveling man goes on the road to take orders, and Hercules went on the road to take the goods.

The next trip for Hercules was a wild goose chase over the face of the earth looking for the golden apples of the Hesperides. These were the apples which Juno had presented to her on her wedding day by some goddess to whom Juno had perhaps been good when she was sick. Juno left these apples with the daughters of Hesperia and a dragon for safe keeping. This dragon was a very fierce looking monster with fangs eighteen inches long, and every time it breathed the air turned green. Hercules found his way over into some part of Africa to a place called Mount Atlas. Atlas was one of the Indians who had met defeat in a war with the gods, and had been sentenced to hold up the weight of the heavens for life. He was the father of Hesperides, and Hercules got an idea into his head that if there was a person on earth who could dig up those apples it was Atlas. Just how to get Atlas from his post was a conundrum hard to crack, as he had to stay on watch all the while and hold up the heavens. Hercules told Atlas that if he would skip out and get the apples he would hold up the heavens while he was gone, providing he did not stay too long. Atlas told him he would be glad of the chance to get a little rest, as holding up the weight of the heavens day and night was no snap. So Atlas went after the golden pippins and brought them to Hercules. He came very near not coming back, however, as it was a great relief to him to get out from under the heavens and rest up a spell. He thought very seriously of throwing up the job and of letting Hercules keep it the rest of his days; however, he returned and shouldered the heavens again and let Hercules go home with the apples.

There lived a giant of the name of Antaeus, who claimed that he was the best catch-as-catch-can wrestler on earth. The reason he made this claim was because he was all right as long as he kept his feet on the ground, but as soon as he was lifted into the air,—exit power. He compelled all strangers who happened into his country to wrestle with him; and also sign a contract that if they were conquered they had to be clubbed to death. Eurystheus told Hercules to go over into that country and sic himself onto Antaeus. So Hercules met the noted wrestler and told him to square off and get ready to die. Antaeus gave Hercules the horse laugh. Hercules did not know about Antaeus having glue on his feet so he could stick to the earth and keep his magic power in good shape. Anyway, Hercules went at him and threw him to the ground easy enough, but he got up each time with renewed strength. When Hercules got next to his secret, he went at him on other lines. He simply picked him up,

HE DID NOT WANT HERCULES TO SEE THE TRACKS OF THE CATTLE AND HE DRAGGED THEM INTO HI
CAVE BY THEIR TAILS.

tossed him into the air, and before he could holler enough, Hercules got in his sure thing work, and choked him until his air valves refused to work, and the light of a great wrestler flickered for the last time.

There was another giant of the name of Cacus, who was a high-class horse thief, and would steal anything he could get his hands on. He lived in a cave in one of the seven hills of Rome. He cultivated a desire for dragging off other people's plunder and was the most noted porch climber in all Rome. He would just as soon steal a grave-stone as to rob an apple woman. He was simply terrible, and the people dreaded him as much as a United States marshal dreads a squirrel rifle in the hands of an Arkansaw moonshiner.

Hercules came along that way one day with a drove of cattle and camped near the cave of Cacus. After Hercules had fallen asleep, Cacus slipped into his camp and took away some of his cattle. He did not want Hercules to see the tracks of the cattle and he dragged them into his cave by their tails, so Hercules would think they had gone in the opposite direction. This was a very clever piece of stratagem on the part of Cacus and Hercules was very sore. He knew not how to recover his lost cattle, and he started on with what he had. As he passed the cave, he heard his lost cows lowing therein. He went in and introduced himself to Cacus, and told him that he was very sorry, but that he would be compelled to punish him for taking away his cattle without leaving his address. He told him that he would make the punishment as light as he could, and he kept his word, for the lightest punishment that Hercules ever carried with him was choking to death, and Cacus got that dose.

Hercules had to take a trip to the infernal regions at one time, but he did not go alone. He took Mercury and the wise unconquered virgin Minerva with him in case he got a bluff down there which he could not call. He got permission from Pluto to take Cerberus back to earth again with a promise that he would not use his club. This Cerberus was a monster with saw teeth and tail feathers. He was hard to curry and was never known to take the bit or stand for a crupper. Hercules did not care for that, nor did he care whether he would stand without being hitched or not, or whether he worked on the off or near side. He went to take him and he took him. Cerberus made an awful struggle, but in vain. Hercules took him to Eurystheus, and then returned him to Pluto without raising his club.

This time, while Hercules was in Hades, he made a hit with Pluto, and got his old friend, Theseus, his imitator and admirer, liberated. He had been held a prisoner for some time for an unsuccessful attempt to kidnap Proserpine.

Hercules had a very good disposition. He was no hand to pick a fuss, but one day he forgot himself. In a fit of anger he took his friend Iphitus by the throat and choked him into eternal silence. This was uncalled for, and Hercules got properly punished. He was made the slave of Queen Omphale for three years. After he served his sentence doing chores he was united in marriage with Dejanira. They lived together three years in perfect peace. Well she knew how strong he was and she thought it policy to keep quiet and live in peace, as it did not pay to kick up a rumpus with a man like him. He asked his wife one day if she would like to take an outing. She replied that she would.

While on their trip through the country, they came to a river. Then they met one of those flea-bitten Centaurs with chin whiskers who called himself Nessus. He was

HE GAVE HIS CLUB TO A FRIEND, STRETCHED HIS TIRED BODY ON LOGS AND REQUESTED HIS FRIEND TO APPLY A MATCH.

doing a ferry business at so much per. Hercules forded the river, but told his wife that she could ride across on the Centaur's back. He crossed over to the opposite side, and all at once the Centaur took a fool notion that he would like to elope with the fair Mrs. Dejanira Hercules, and he started on the dead run down the river bank. Hercules heard his wife's cries, and the first thing he thought of was to overtake the Centaur and choke him, but the latter was too swift, so Hercules shot an arrow into the Centaur's heart and that settled it. Before he had breathed his last he told Dejanira to take some of his blood and keep it in a cool place, as she could use it as a charm to keep her husband's love in good order. She took the blood and kept it, and it was not long until she got a notion in her head that she ought to try it. Hercules while at war in a foreign country took a maiden of the name of Iole prisoner. He seemed very fond of her, his wife thought.

When he was about to give a grand time in honor of his big battles, he sent to his wife for a white robe to use in the parade. She thought it a good chance to try the love spell business, so she soaked the robe in the Centaur's blood. She then washed out the stain and sent it to her husband. He put it on and as soon as he got warmed up the poison got into his system and it caused him such pain that it broke up the parade. In his awful agony he seized Lichas,—the messenger who had brought the robe to him—and hurled him seven miles out into the sea. He lighted so heavily that it broke his contract. Hercules attempted to wrench the robe from his body, but it stuck to his hide, and when he tore it off great chunks of flesh came with it. In this condition he boarded a schooner and sailed for home. Dejanira saw what a bad break she had made and she felt so badly about it that she lynched herself.

Hercules got ready to die. He climbed to the top of Mount Aetna and there he made a funeral pyre of logs. He gave his club to a friend, stretched his tired body on logs and requested his friend to apply a match. Jupiter took charge of him then and sent him up among the stars in a four-horse rig. When he arrived, Atlas knew it, as he felt the weight of heaven increase. Hercules got a great reception up there and made a decided hit with Juno's daughter, Miss Hebe, and married her. She was a young thing and the goddess of youth. Hercules, however, knew that before he married her.

More might be said of Hercules, but as he is in heaven now I hate to disturb him, for I know he would not have stood for it down here, and perhaps he does not like to up there.

IF I HAD A MILLION.

F I HAD a million I would plough the deep heaving seas until I found an island that suited me; then I would buy it and set myself up as King. I would not be a haughty King. I would treat my subjects well as long as they behaved. I would wear plough shoes and yarn galluses just to please them. I would not care to be a great builder of temples and cities like King Rameses II. I had rather spend the money for pies, shortcake and stick candy for the natives. If I had to tax my people to build fine temples, then they would all be poor. I would not have the heart to watch them shake their breakfasts off the tropical trees. It would be inconsistent with my pastoral nature. A full stomach is far better than much gazing at fine temples.

The hasty progress of man is the progress of sin, destruction, desolation, wickedness, riots, brimstone and rheumatism. The conservative man who is not in a rush to build an annex to his hen-house until he can afford it is not guilty of hasty progress, and he will stand a good chance of getting three meals each day.

Where one man grows rich in a real estate boom, forty-nine will go broke. I was in that business twelve years, and all I have to show for it is a lot of gray hairs and the gout. But I am leaving my text.

I remind myself of a Methodist preacher who was our circuit rider for a number of years in Arkansaw. The last time I heard him preach he commenced at the tenth chapter of Isaiah and wound up in the siege of Sebastapol.

I say, if I had a million I would call my kingdom the Isle of Rest. I would build me a palace of brick and mortar. The walls should be ten cubits thick so I could not hear sad reports of bloodshed from other lands. I would have the roof painted a sky blue, and there would be vines on all sides. The woodshed would be fixed the same way.

The front yard of the place would be a tangled wild-wood of weeping willows, giant palms, sycamores, cedars and dogwood. I would have six fountains of wonderful size, something on the order of a Yellowstone Park geyser. These fountains would be in constant eruption, spouting forth the richest nectar that ever touched the lips of man. One would spout gin fizzes. That I would call the fountain of morn. Another would spout milk punches, the fountain of human kindness. Another would spout mint juleps, the fountain of hospitality. Another would spout old rye with seltzer, the fountain of sunshine. Another would spout sherry and eggs, the fountain of youth. The sixth one would spout champagne, the fountain of joy, laughter and song.

I would use the back yard in which to store cord wood, the ash hopper, chicken coops and kettles to be used on wash days. I would put up with nothing but home cooking. I would eat poultry, pudding, papaws and pie. I would order a forty-horse biscuit dipped in sausage gravy. When I had company at the palace I would wear seal skin pants and satin socks. I would have my swimming pool filled with dew from the morning lilies. Everything would be to the King's taste. I would have a garden of softest verdure covered with pansy blossoms, sweet violets and Johnnie-jump-ups. I would also have an extra garden with nothing growing there but clover, that would be for the King to roll in. If a mortgage and loan man should come to me and offer to loan money on the palace I would call my guards and have him mummified at sunrise. I would have a hunting ground, where no one but the King could hunt, as I am fond of the chase. I do not mean the kind of chasing so common in this country. I would have the game trained so that when any animal saw me coming it would stand still and get shot. Of course, that would be pot shooting, but there would be no one to kick about it but the King.

I would never have a swelled head just because I was a King, then my crown would always fit me.

The laws of my kingdom would be plain and simple. I would be the court of justice and the lord high executioner. I would appoint a sufficient number of officers to keep the Isle of Rest quiet. This would suit me better than a free country or a republican form of government. Not that I am at all opposed to a free country, but vulgar elections would be avoided. Then if there was any robbing the Kingdom to be done I would do it.

I would be an anti-expansionist, unless I wanted another island or two, and that would be different.

My divorce laws would be a snap. If a man and his wife came to me and told me that they had decided to separate I would tell them to proceed at once and sep-

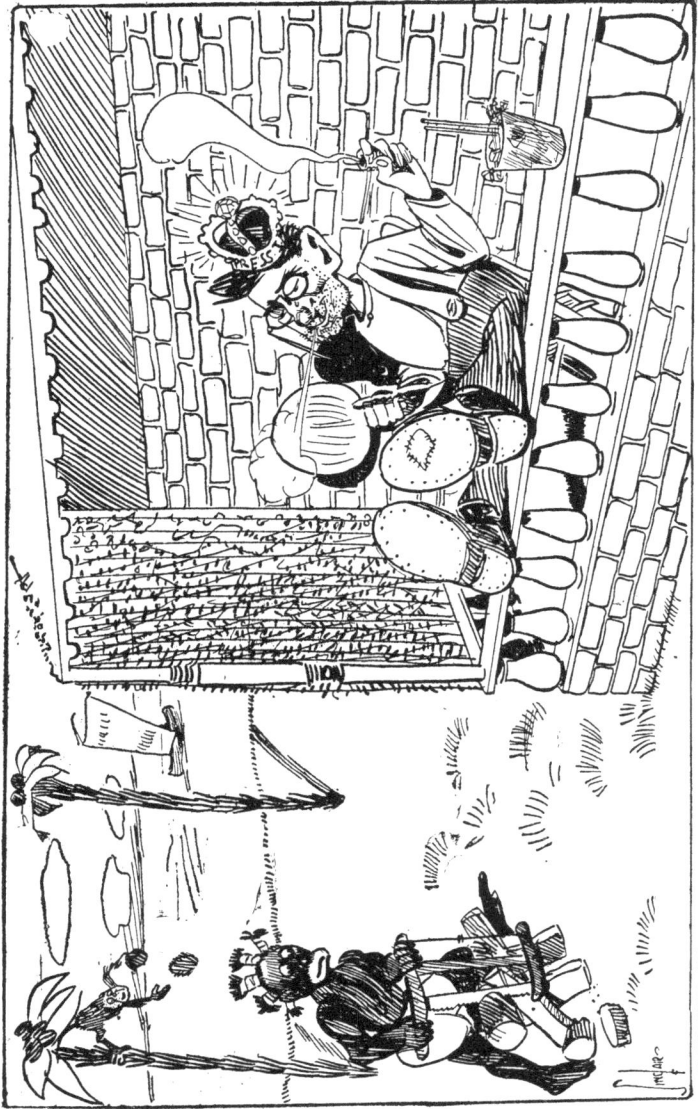

I WOULD NEVER HAVE A SWELLED HEAD JUST BECAUSE I WAS A KING, THEN MY CROWN WOULD ALWAYS FIT ME.

arate. I do not believe that a man and his wife should be forced to remain man and wife just to please the law. A law that forces unnecessary unhappiness would not be practiced by the King of the Isle of Rest. If a man and his wife are not mated and are unhappy, then let one fly east and the other fly west. It is a sin to put a monkey and a parrot together in the same cage. They are incompatibles and to force them to live together is a mean trick.

When the summer's work was done and the corn was in the crib, I would advertise for a queen. I would not want a queen with golden curls and eyes like diamonds and all that business the poets sing about. I would want just a plain sort of a queen to lend dignity to the palace and to her lord and master. I would want one who was not curious, suspicious or jealous, one who would not rubber at another woman as she passed and say:

"Oh, I don't know, she aint so much."

If she was guilty of these offenses at any time I would separate her from her title and get her a job at plain sewing. I would then advertise for another queen.

If people from foreign lands should come to the Isle of Rest and show their dislike for the laws, by making inflammatory political speeches, I would have them imprisoned for forty days under a tub. Then I would send them forty miles out to sea on a raft and have them turned adrift.

The Isle of Rest would have freedom of religion absolutely. There are so many things on this earth which come high that I believe salvation should be on the free list. Let every man take the religion he chooses, whether it be ethical or otherwise.

Emigration would not be tolerated unless every person over twelve could read, write, spell and work examples in arithmetic as far over as long division. Besides each one should have 1,000 shekels, so if I did not like their style I could tax them clean off the Island.

I would do a great many other things, if I had a million. I would be generous with my friends, and other people's friends. I would dress up and look wise, and laugh all the time. It would be a safe bet, if I had a million, that in one year I would be broke.

ON THE BATTLEFIELD.

THIS is a story I tell every year between July and eternity. The reason I tell it is because I have told it so many times I believe it. If I should hear anyone else tell it I would not believe it. I do not believe that anyone would take chances on telling it. It is safe to say that they would not make a hit with it. I never did. Telling stories is a funny business. If you tell a story and it falls flat, you feel no larger than four cents; at least that is the case with me.

A friend once told me a story that happened in the section of Arkansaw where I was raised.

"Down on the St. Louis & San Francisco railroad," he said, "there was an eating station which was very much Arkansaw. About all one could get there was smoked hog's jowl cooked with greens, lye hominy and middling meat. One day I was going through that section on a local passenger train. A brakeman came through the cars yelling out:

" 'Next station! twenty minutes for dinner.'

"As we rolled into the depot I could smell the bacon. An old white-haired negro stood out in front of the building ringing a bell for all he was worth. Near him sat one of those yellow, hungry-looking Arkansaw dogs with his eyes closed and his face turned heavenward, howling and crying at the clanging of the bell. As I passed through the door the negro stopped and looking down at the dog said:

" 'Lookey harh, dog! what's yo' cryin' 'bout? Yo' don't haft ter eat hash."

Now, of course, when he told that story I had to laugh. That same evening I told the same story to a friend, and he never even smiled. All I could do was to look and feel foolish. I met him the next day, and he said to me:

"Do you remember that story you told me last evening?"

"I do; what about it?"

"Well, why didn't that negro feed that dog?"

Early in the Spring, twenty-two years ago, I was overtaken with a morbid desire to rent a farm. I lived at that time in Pendleton, Oregon. I wanted to get away from the song of the blacksmith's anvil. The noise of town made me nervous. I met a man (whose name I have forgotten, and I guess he is glad of it) who owned a farm on Birch Creek, eighteen miles south of Pendleton. He said he would rent me his farm, allowing me half the crop and half the apples and grapes. I accepted his offer right there and then, and took charge of the farm at once.

The least I could figure on making that season was $5,000. I also figured out what I could do with the money when I got it. I felt that I had a new lease on life, and I could not see anything ahead of me but sunshine and wealth.

In due time I found myself on that farm ready for business. The first thing I discovered was that I had to live alone and do my own cooking. There was only a brindle dog to keep me company, and he had the least sense of any dog I had ever met. Every time I started to sing he would cry. I could not blame him for that, for I had tried my singing on men and women and they would not stand for it. He would stay out all night in the rain; then in the morning he would come in soaking wet whining for a drink.

The nights were very lonesome, and the coyotes made things all the more hideous with their unearthly howls. I believe there are more coyotes to the square acre in that part of Oregon than any other place on earth. As for keeping batch, I made a botch of it. My cooking was very plain. I ate boiled potatoes until I had a brogue, and the egg habit fastened itself onto me, so that I hated to hear a hen sing. The very sight of a chicken was repulsive to me.

I started in ploughing early so that I could get my crop in and get it off my mind. Everything went along very well. I put in ten acres of garden truck and it all came up fine. I could not have asked for better prospects. As time wore on, I could see very plainly that if it did not rain soon everything I had would wilt and dry up. The parching sun poured down its scorching rays day after day. I kept on eating potatoes and eggs and praying for rain. The long drouth disheartened me, but the worst was yet to come. The first thing I knew a grasshopper plague set in. They came by the millions, settled on that ranch and took everything that looked green. Then I quit praying for rain. I made up my mind to turn the farm over to the grasshoppers, which I did. I was then ready to pack up and return to Pendleton.

One morning I looked across the field and saw a man and a woman running for their lives. Something terrible had happened I was certain. As they neared the house I ran out and opened the gate for them. They reached the place exhausted and frightened half to death. Almost out of breath the man said:

"For God's sake, man! do you know the danger you are in? Hitch up your team as quick as possible and let us fly for our lives to Pendleton. The Bannock Indians are on the warpath, and they are butchering settlers all over the country. Wife and I just escaped being slaughtered by the red devils. Make all haste with your team or they will overtake us and we will be shot down like dogs."

For a few seconds I was speechless, and turned blind with fright. I told him to send his wife in the house, then help me hitch up the team. We rushed out to the barn, and in a short time we were ready to fly to safety. I can never forget how that poor woman suffered with fear. We all piled into the wagon and pulled out for Pendleton. The road was good, the horses in fine trim and there was no excuse for slow time. To say the least, we were not long in reaching our destination. We found Pendleton wild with excitement. The town was fortified with sacks of wool, wagons, fence rails and everything and anything that would turn an Indian bullet. There was a large stone flouring mill in the upper end of town, and in that all the women and children were harbored. Pendleton was situated on the edge of the Umatilla reservation, and the people were afraid that the Umatilla Indians would join the Bannocks. In such an event saltpeter would not have saved us.

All day wagons loaded with dead and dying settlers were pouring into town. The wailing of the grief-

THE ROAD WAS GOOD, THE HORSES IN FINE TRIM AND THERE WAS NO EXCUSE FOR SLOW TIME.

stricken mothers and wives was something terrible. They were running from one neighbor's house to another telling of the awful fate that had befallen their brothers, sons or husbands. It was an impressive scene that I can never forget, and I hope never to see such another. It seemed that the situation was growing worse every hour. Volunteers had gone to the front, and more were to follow. There were but few guns and little ammunition left. I had never seen an Indian on the warpath, and every time I saw my shadow I would shy off to one side like a frightened horse. I had never read about Indians, as the only books we had on the farm were the family Bible and Doctor Chase's recipe book.

I got in everybody's way somehow. I never felt so out of place in my life. I learned that a number of volunteers were getting ready to leave the next day. I was well aware of the fact that horses were about as scarce as guns, and that pleased me, for if there was one place on earth that I did not care to go it was to the front. I had never been introduced to the Bannock Indians, and I did not care to go into the hills and pick a row with them. I wanted the volunteers to think I was anxious to go, however, and that taking Indian scalps was sport for me. In order to carry out my bluff I went to a prominent attorney, whose name was Jim Turner, (now deceased, alas!) and I timidly said to him:

"I do wish I had a horse; I would like to join that company of volunteers and go to Willow Springs with them."

"A horse! is that all that's holding you?"

"Yes, sir; if I could only get a horse I——"

"Well, don't let that bother you. You see that bald face horse tied to the court house fence?"

"Ye, ye, yes, sir; I see him."

"Well, that is my horse, and you can take him."

"No, no, Mr. Turner; I did not mean to say that—that I could go; you see I have a-a-er friend, and he——"

"Oh, yes, of course, you have a friend now you want to go. I suppose you made the bluff that you wanted to go because you thought there were no horses to be had?"

"Ye, yes, no, no, not exactly that; you see this friend is an old Indian fighter and he is very anxious to——"

"Oh, well, now stop your bluffing and take my horse and go on."

"Yes, sir, oh yes, sir, I will go; I want to go, but I wanted to give my friend the preference, as he wants to to——"

"Stay here—I guess, just the same as you do, but you will both go, if I know myself."

"Yes, sir, we will both go, but I wanted to be good to him. I will take your horse and beat my friend to the fighting line if I can."

That was one of the times I got brave at the wrong place. I was in for it; I had to go with the volunteers early the next morning. I retired early that night with a heavy heart. I did a great deal of reflecting, regretting and thinking before I fell asleep. I saw myself on the battlefield fighting desperately. We made a charge upon a thousand Indians or more. In this struggle I saw myself fall from my horse with a mortal wound in my breast. I was carried from the field on a stretcher. I could see my cold form in a casket with friends around me. The remains were shipped back to the dear ones at home who had always loved and cherished me. I saw them lift the casket cover and take a farewell look at the brave boy who fell on the battlefield fighting for his country. Then I heard the dead march, and they followed the casket to the silent grave on the little mound in the cemetery, where

others had gone before me.   I saw them all as they stood
by that lonely grave, shedding tears and weeping for a
mother's boy who had left them never to return.   I
thought of the flight of the soul and was wondering
when I would join the heavenly band, when I heard a
loud knock at my door and the order:

"Say, 'Lengthy,' you tenderfoot, climb out of there.
It's four o'clock; Captain Berry and his men are about
ready to start."

I had passed a wretched night, and I wished with all
my soul that Jim Turner's horse would drop dead.   The
drouth and the grasshoppers had taken my crop, and I
did not care to finish up the summer by allowing a lot
of wild, blood-thirsty Indians to take me.

Five minutes before our Captain gave the sign of distress—to move on, I was in the saddle.   Thirty-five of
the bravest volunteers that ever shouldered guns on the
Umatilla river started on a forty-mile march.   That old
horse of mine looked more like a saw-horse than a war-
horse.   I promptly named him Cultus, which in the
Chinook jargon means positively no good.   He had but
two shoes, and one of them was loose.   He was lame in
one leg, and every time he struck a trot I went up and
down in the saddle like a churn dasher.   My stirrup
straps were much too short; this added to my misery.
I certainly presented the picture of a sad looking warrior.
I did not even look the part of self defense.   Cultus was
a slow beast, always a hundred feet or so behind the
others.   Beating him did little good.   He seemed as in-
vulnerable as a log.   Between holding my gun, whipping
that horse and jumping up and down in my saddle, I was
about the busiest soldier in the company.

The truth of it is, I did not know how to ride a horse.
All the rehearsing I ever had up to that time was in go-

I DID NOT EVEN LOOK THE PART OF SELF DEFENSE.

ing to an old watermill with a turn of corn on a plough
mule down south.   I never had a profession that I could
brag on, so it is safe to presume that I felt embarrassed
with these volunteers.

We pushed on hour after hour toward the field of
destruction.   I did not ask many questions, as my com-
panions were inclined to poke fun at me.   Every little
while some of the boys would look back at the cloud of
dust which surrounded me and yell:

"Hurry up there, tenderfoot, or you will get lost."

I was such a long, lean, hungry looking pair of tongs
that it really seemed a pity to take me out to be shot full
of holes by a lot of wild redskins.   I knew that I could
never hit an Indian, even if I had one tied to a tree, and
I also knew that if we had to retreat the other volunteers
would make their escape and I would be captured, because Cultus was so slow.

We traveled all day through the boiling sun which
poured down like fiery beams from Sheol, and never saw
an Indian.   We did meet, however, a great many settlers fleeing for their lives toward Pendleton with their
dead and wounded.   They told us of the awful depreda-
tions of the Indians.   Settlers had been shot down and
then cut to pieces.   Many of them had been pinned to
the earth and left to die by inches.   Some had been
scalped and tortured in a most fiendish manner.   Women
and children were crying and weeping over the bodies of
their kindred.   One man dashed up to us on his horse
almost crazed with excitement.

"For God's sake, men!" he said, "don't attempt to
go to Willow Springs with that handful of volunteers!
You will all be massacred!   Not one of you will live to
tell the story."

I DID NOT MIND BEING SHOT AT, ONLY THEY WERE SO CARELESS AND ROUGH ABOUT IT.

223

All we met begged us not to go any farther without reinforcements. Of course, these stories did not quiet my nerves. I was then about ready to fall off my horse with fear. Our Captain took no heed of the advice given him. He said he could take thirty-five men and kill off hundreds of Indians, and on we went. When we reached Willow Springs I was tired, hungry and saddlesore. We staked our horses, lighted a camp fire and prepared a meal. Our Captain gave us orders how to act in case we should be attacked that night. There was a sheep-shed near by and we spread our blankets and turned in for the night. The next morning at daybreak the roof of the shed was perforated with bullets. There was a perfect shower of them, and in thirty minutes it resembled a porous plaster. On the top of a hill to the east of us the Indians had fortified themselves while we slept. I did not mind being shot at, only they were so careless and rough about it. Our Captain gave a rush order:

"Out of this shed, face in line and shoot for all you are worth."

All was confusion, and, of course, I got in everybody's way. Somehow I was the last man out of that shed, although from my double quick movements they all thought I would be the first out, the first in line, and the first to get killed. When we lined up it reminded me of the first spelling class in a country school, some toed in and some toed out. Just then there must have been another army of Indians turned loose, for there was a regular hail storm of lead. The bullets came down like rain drops in the dust. We returned the fire as fast as we could load, although we could not see the enemy. Once in a while one or two Indians would venture down the backbone of the hill. We could not see much of them, however, as they hid behind their horses.

Charley Hendricks jumped into the air and said: "Well, they got me," and he limped over toward the shed with a wound in his left leg. In another minute two more of our men, Hale and LeMar, were mortally wounded and fell dead. Our horses were suffering, and as the Captain saw we were in a tight place he gave the order to retreat. We took the bodies of the two dead men, lashed them to their horses, and got out of there faster than we went in. I do not know just how many Indians we were fighting, but from the way they whooped and yelled and fired it seemed to me there must have been between 3,000,000 and 4,000,000. As we were leaving Cultus received a shot in the hip. It was certainly the most awakening thing that ever happened to him. He acted like an Arabian steed, and tried to run away with me. I let him run, but not too far ahead, as I did not know how soon I might run into a fresh band of Bannocks. We had been retreating for something like an hour, when it occurred to me that my left foot was very hot. I had on boots, and as I looked down at the left one I discovered a bullet hole at the ankle, from which there was oozing a stream of blood. Here my heart almost failed me, because I was certain I only had a few moments to live. I was sure that my whole being was soaked with bullets. My sad whine was pitiful.

The boys took me off my horse, and removed my boot. In the battle there was one bullet I did not dodge and I got it in the ankle, but on account of the excitement I did not feel the pain at that time. I did not care so much about the ankle wound, but in an excited manner I begged the boys to take off my shirt and see how many times I was shot in the body. They examined me, but could find no other wound. I felt some easier then, so I mounted old Cultus and we were off.

On the road home we saw an Indian scout at a distance. One of our boys took steady aim, and poor Lo's untutored mind saw a spirit in the clouds and heard something in the winds,—then his glim went out. This is only a polite way of saying that he shot that scout between the eyes and killed him deader than a nit.

When we reached Pendleton, I rode up to the court house fence and tied Cultus right where I got him. Then I walked lame to Jim Turner's office and told him that I could find a friend to take his horse if he would see about getting me on the pension list.

Since that time I have never spoken of Indians, unless I know they are dead; then my remarks are kindly, but I don't mean them.

ROOSTERS.

OR many years I have made a careful study of the rooster. He, of course, belongs to the ornithological kingdom because he is a bird, but he has many of the traits and idiosyncrasies of mankind. He is gregarious as long as there is a hen left in the barnyard. In company with a bevy of hens, he is always garrulous, polite, pleasing, ostentatious, brave, arrogant, jealous, deceitful, and very much of a flirt. With his hypnotic power he is able to wield a great influence; should that power fail him he resorts to coercion. If he is a game rooster, he makes an effort to exercise a rigorous sway over all the scrub birds on the place. In short, he tries to hold supreme command, and this he can never do until he puts a lot of his opponents to sleep in a few unfriendly bouts. When a light or middle-weight rival, whose spurs and fetlocks are not up to date, crosses the game rooster's path he gives him one withering look, as if to say:

"I am the invincible. This means for you servitude, a sore head and a new roosting place if you pester around my covey."

In the early morning I have been seated on the barnyard fence and have watched with interest the æsthetic

rooster in his peregrinations. His whole aim and study
seems to be on how to make a hit with the hens. He is
to be complimented on his subtleties and subterfuges. I
have seen him saunter over to one corner of the yard with
devilment in his eyes and deceitfulness in his walk.
There he would scratch around until he found a bit of
something to eat, which he was careful not to swallow.
He would pick it up, then let it drop, repeating the performance several times, all the while calling to the hens
to come running. He would make such a fuss about it
that the hens thought perhaps he had found a diamond,
and they just fell all over each other getting to him. I
imagined that when he was making all the noise about
his find he was saying to the hens:

"Gee whiz! girls, come in a rush! I have found
breakfast for all; hurry up! See which one of you can
get here first."

Just about the time they came up he would deftly
swallow the bit of food. Then he would look at them
with a smile of blandishment and as much as to say:

"Well, I fooled you that time, didn't I?"

All the hens could do then was to stand around and
look foolish. Then to add insult to injury, he would
walk around with his big feet and step on some hen's foot
every time. Perhaps, it would not be ten minutes until
he would be in another corner of the yard and play
the same joke over again on the same hens. It made
little difference how many times a day he played this
favorite joke of his, the hens never failed to run to him
and see what he had found. It occurred to me that he
must be the official joker of the barnyard, and that they
simply ran to him to carry out the joke, or something of
that kind. Perhaps it was because everything female is
susceptible of deception.

HE WOULD MAKE SUCH A FUSS ABOUT IT THAT THE HENS THOUGHT
PERHAPS HE HAD FOUND A DIAMOND.

The life of a hen is by no means a happy one.   When she is not being deceived by some low browed rooster, she is employing her time on a setting of eggs.   It is no wonder that a setting hen gets cross.   She sets and sets until she is all worn out and as stiff as a poker for the want of exercise and fresh air.   A rooster would let her set there for nine years before he would offer to take a shift keeping her eggs warm.   He is always too busy trifling.   Now a canary bird is different.   The male will take a regular shift and give the little hen a chance to shake herself and take a bath, besides while she is on watch he will take her something to eat like any rooster should.   A poor old sad-eyed hen, however, will set on eggs or door-knobs until her nerves are wrecked and her disposition ruined forever, and never receive the least attention.   No wonder they scold.   I used to imagine that a setting hen could swear and use cuss words in her own language.   I am now convinced I was right.

A gentleman ostrich will take turn about on a setting of eggs.   When the hen grows tired the male relieves her while she takes a rest and at the same time eats up a keg of nails and a few oyster cans.   Some writer has said that the ostrich leaves its eggs on the sands of the desert to be hatched by the heat of the sun.   That might have been the case in that writer's time, but the ostrich of to-day is different.

Pliny the Elder in speaking of the ostrich said :

"They imagine when they have thrust their head and neck into a bush that the whole of the body is concealed."

If Mr. Pliny was living he could guess again, as the modern ostrich has cut that out, especially those in the circus business.

He also said that roosters prelude their crowing by clapping their wings on their sides.   He has another guess on that also. The noise is produced by the clapping of their wings together over their backs. Anyone who wishes to satisfy himself on this point can set up all night and watch for the prelude of a rooster's crowing at the break of day. What has worried me most about a rooster is that he can go on in the practice of deception, never rendering the least assistance and still the hens all stand for it. The only thing about roosters worthy of mention is that they are good about announcing the coming of day. Even at that I have heard them crow all night just to mislead a chickenless farmer.

ANSWERING CORRESPONDENCE.

F late I have received a number of letters from persons seeking information. The following letter reached my office yesterday.

DEAR SIR: Would you be kind enough to answer a few very important questions for me? I am about to be married to a young man whose name is Willis. The wedding will take place right after haying time. I want you to give me some ideas about my bridal suit and second-day dress. What material do you think would look cute and innocent-like, and how do you think it should be made up? It will be the first time I was ever married and I am so nervous that I do not know half the time where I am. I am told that you are a married man, and I would like to have you advise me how a husband should be treated to insure domestic happiness. I would like also to know how he should treat me, because I have made up my mind squaretoed and flat-footed that no man can ever run over me if I know myself.

Willis is very affectionate and has chestnut brown hair. I have found one objection to him; he is somewhat hyperbolical, and that I despise in anyone. He is tall and does not care for expenses. He has no trade or profession, but he can do most anything that is lucrative. At present he is digging wells, but I do not like to have him work at that. I had rather have him do something where he can be on earth, as working under ground is dangerous. He is liable to get full of gas and leave a widow to mourn his loss. He has shoveled coal, worked in a bath house, herded sheep, pulled corn, hung wall paper and broke up ground. He would have broke up his father also if he could have had his way. Being familiar with all this work, I can not see why he should experience any trouble in supporting me. Of course, I could help to earn the living, only I swore once that I would never work out.

I love him half to death and will do almost anything to make him happy, although I will never allow him to mistreat me. If he ever does, I will put turpentine in his coffee, sprinkle him with dish-water all over and then sic the dogs on him. I have heard ma-ma talk about men, and she says if a woman gives in to her husband he will treat her meaner than an ash-cat. I haven't much education, but I do consider that I have a little horse-sense.

Willis is of a good family, except that his father comes home once in a while fuller than a fiddler and acts terribly. If his temper happens to be bad he will tear up the carpets, put out all the fires and then go out into the orchard and pull up young fruit trees. And his breath, gee whiz! it would put the organ out of tune.

As soon as we are married, we will take a short bridal tour. Willis has suggested that we go out camping.

I am 35 years old, weigh 191 pounds, have short blonde hair and am fond of ice cream and fruit cake.

Please answer as soon as you can conveniently and give me all the information possible, as I hope you recognize the fact that we women do not have the attention and care we should have—hence the need of information.

Yours truly,   JANE.

P. S.—Do you know how to make good corn bread? If so, please send me a recipe; also give me some points on how to raise chickens. I would like to know also whether you believe in hoodoos and signs. Willis is just full of them. Yours,   J.

DEAR MISS JANE: Your favor of late date has been read, and I shall endeavor to give you enough information to enable you to stand your ground if Willis should at any time go on the warpath.

Now, of course, Miss Jane, I must tell you right on the jump that I am not a married man. I was once engaged to be married to a maiden fair, however, but her parents registered a kick, and her brothers were opposed to it. At last she backed out and I quit. So for some reason we did not get married. She told me that she would never marry me anyway, unless I had enough money put away to pay for a divorce suit. I kind of took it for granted that she did not anticipate a happy marriage, so she returned the engagement ring and I went to work in a saw-mill.

I do not know how to make good corn-bread; I tried it once on the farm, and when it was ready to eat it looked like petrified bark. It would have made a very good door prop.

I hope you and your Willis will be a big success, and you can be if you know how to handle him. I may say here, however, that I think marriage east of the Missouri river is a failure.

You say Willis has chestnut brown hair and that yours is of a blonde color. That ought to be a good combination, but if you fail to agree you will find him a chestnut and you will be red-headed more than once. If you take pains and study him you will soon learn how to emulsify the corrugated edges of his coarse nature.

You say he is somewhat hyperbolical. I am sorry for that, for if he is given to stumbling over the truth while he is single there is no telling where he will stop after he is married. A great many married men cultivate the habit of telling falsehoods. I never could understand why they do it, but they do. If a man had to wash his mouth with soap every time he told an untruth his neighbors would think from his looks that he was in the habit of eating suds.

When you are married to Willis, the first thing to do is to get the names of all his friends. You need not ask him who they are, for sooner or later he will tell you. Keep them all in mind, and do not show at any time that you are suspicious, but give him plenty of rope. The time will come when he will tell you about being out with Jim the night before, and it may turn out that Jim has been out of town all Summer. Then you can make your husband look like a cripple.

The husband business is a great problem. It is true they are indispensable, and yet they often ship in trainloads of unhappiness for a tender, loving and defenseless wife to stack up in the front parlor of a little home. Where mirth and joy should reign in her heart, there is a great cargo of misery. Her affections are lacerated and her bright hopes have turned to extreme anguish.

The clouds above are no longer sprinkling pots of heaven, sending down showers of crystal drops to cool the burning earth. They are simply tears of worm-wood, nothing more. I am more than sure, however, that this will never be the case with your Willis. Should he turn out to be that kind of a husband I would advise you not to argue with him, but just quietly go out into the backyard and get the ax. That is a fetcher. There is not one husband in a hundred thousand who is not afraid of an ax in the hands of a woman. They are so awkward something sad is sure to happen. The double bitted ax is the best. Of course, I do not recommend you to put your husband on the shelf for good, but you might make him walk lame.

I am glad to know that Willis does not drink. Strong drink is a dangerous thing for a married man to dally with. Indulgence is followed up with anger, ill-will, sorrow, grief, excessive care and whiskey gout. It is your province to exercise a proper control over your husband and keep him from drink. Deep-seated love is the first thing. Make him love you by being ever constant. Love is free. No combination will ever get a corner on it. Love is the divine essence of your whole system. The statesman is the leader of a nation; the warrior is the grace of an age; the philosopher is the birth of a whole lot of things; but the lover, oh! where is he not? So do not forget to love your husband from Xmas to Xmas. In return he will love you the same, and look upon strong drink as he would a viper.

It is a husband's duty to build fires in the cook stove, and to assist his wife every possible way. It is such little things as peeling potatoes, grinding coffee, filling the water kettle, scrubbing the kitchen floor, putting out Monday's washing, blacking the stoves, beating carpets, washing dishes, and getting the children to bed that makes a wife open the door of her heart, and causes her eyes to gleam with purest love.

You should never allow your husband to look into the sewing machine drawer. It is liable to make him shift-less. The usual inventory of a sewing machine drawer runs something like this: a lot of hooks and eyes tangled up with silk twist and candle-snuffers; scraps of dress goods, love letters, gas bills, oil cans, hat pins, zephyrs, shoe laces, buttons, whale bones, corset steels, buckles, thread, hairpins, toilet soap and curling irons. When a man has pawed over this mess he is keyed up to per-form almost any desperate deed.

Domestic rows should be avoided by all means. When you get angry you should go to the ice house and cool off. Every time a man and his wife quarrel they have lost just so many minutes of this life's sun-shine. We have but a few short hours on this cold, wicked ball of dirt, and we should make it a continuous performance of merriment. But, as I said before, in order to keep peace and get your husband on an agree-able basis you may at times be forced to go for the ax.

You say you want some ideas about a bridal suit. I would suggest that you have a neat fitting infant waist, made of some material like dotted swiss or mull, trimmed with valenciennes lace about one-half finger length deep. A cape of ecru Spanish lace will also add to the innocent effect. I would advise you to buy all silk lace if you can·afford it, as lace with a cotton back soon gets nappy, besides it looks a little jakey. A plain straight skirt without gores but with a broad hem would be neat and not fussy. For a second day dress, use one of your old ones. Willis would not know the difference, besides you

would make a hit with your mother-in-law. She would
think more of you for being sensible and economical.

If you insist on raising chickens I would advise you
to find some one thoroughly posted in that business, and
then hire him.

You want to know if I believe in hoodoos and signs.
I must frankly admit that I do. You will remember,
no doubt, when you were a little girl, your father and
mother told you they had found you in a hollow tree
or briar patch, when you were an infant. Your brother
on the doorstep in a basket and your sister in a straw
stack, and so on. My folks told me that they found me
in a brush pile. After I grew up, I made it a point
to examine brush piles and see what I could find in them
besides baby boys. In all my searching I never found
anything but rabbits and the foot of a rabbit is the
worst kind of a hoodoo. There is no telling how long
I was in that brush pile with the rabbits before my folks
found me. That may account for my being a professional hoodoo. I am the official hoodoo of all the middle states.

If I should spread an umbrella in the house some
one would steal it within six hours. It would then
pour down rain for the next three weeks. If I should
attempt to steal an umbrella to get even I would be sure
to get arrested.

When I take a street car it is almost sure to leave
the track.

I have been in four train wrecks, receiving injuries
in each of them. I brought suit against four companies
for damages and never received four cents. I have been
held up on stage coaches three times in California, once
in Arizona and once in Oregon. In three of these
holdups the robbers invited me to give up what I had,

I HAD NO MONEY, BUT THE ROBBERS TOOK MY WATCH AND THEN GAVE ME A GOOD SOUND KICKING FOR BEING BROKE.

The other passengers were not molested.   In the Arizona holdup I had no money but the robbers took my watch and then gave me a good sound kicking for being broke.

In hotel fires I am always the last one to get out with my life, but never save my personal effects.

I started on a tramp steamer from San Francisco to South America some years ago.   When we reached a point about eighty miles off the coast of Guatemala the boat lost its propeller and we drifted at the mercy of the mad sea for three days.   Then the cargo shifted, the vessel sprung a leak, and we had to abandon her before she went down.   We took the lifeboats and rafts and started out to do a credit business—trusting in Providence.   For two days and nights we drifted without food or water.   At last we were picked up by a passing steamer and taken to Callao, Peru.   If the captains of either of these steamers had known that they had a Jonah aboard I would not be here to tell you about it.

I was once a justice of the peace in Oregon and had the pleasure of tying the Gordian knot for three couples while I held that office.   One of the men afterward committed suicide, another was drowned, and the third secured a divorce.   A prisoner was brought before me one day charged with stealing hogs.   I adjudged him guilty and gave him thirty days and costs.   He allowed that the sentence was too severe, and proposed to shake dice with me to see whether I should make the sentence sixty days or nothing.   I agreed.   He shook four aces and I shook a pair of deuces.

I have crossed the continent twelve times and each time with one exception I have been compelled to sleep in an upper berth.   That time I traveled on a tea train and there was no Pullman.

FOR TWO DAYS AND NIGHTS WE DRIFTED WITHOUT FOOD OR WATER.

241

There once stood a farm house near our place in Arkansaw, the owner of which was a bachelor. He died and left the farm to a relative. This relative rented the place to a stranger from Texas. He said the reason he left Texas was because he was hoodooed. On the death of the old bachelor the report went out that the house was haunted. This did not frighten the Texan, however.

The first day he worked about the house cleaning up and getting things in shape. In the evening he sat on the porch, smoked his pipe in comfort and saw nothing. The next night as he sat there, with his legs crossed, enjoying himself, a ghost appeared by his side. He did not wait to argue, but dropped his pipe, jumped the fence and broke across a field for dear life. He ran until he was almost exhausted, and then he sat on a stump, panting like a foxhound. He was not swift enough to get away from that ghost, however. It was at his side in an instant and said to the man from Texas:

"Well, we had quite a chase."

The stranger jumped up with a wild look in his eyes and said to the ghost:

"Yes! and by gosh we will have another chase right now."

The last heard of the Texan was at the crossing of the Arkansaw river and he was then on the move.

I was once billed to lecture in a town out west. The manager of the opera house had written me that every seat was sold for the occasion. When the train pulled into the depot I noticed that the people were wild with excitement. Those who were not running with buckets of water were crying "Fire!" at the top of their voices. As soon as I could collect my thoughts I asked the station agent what building was burning. He said it was the opera house.

HE SHOOK FOUR ACES AND I SHOOK A PAIR OF DUCES.

Thursday is my unlucky day. For all the good I can do on that day I had just as well stay in bed.

An owl came to my window one night and hooted three times. After that I had the typhoid fever for three months.

It is a strange thing to me that I am alive. I guess the only reason I am permitted to live is to teach hoodooism to others.

If Willis is a hoodoo he will remain one as long as he lives and I am truly sorry for him.

I will conclude by asking you to accept all the wishes that go with a wedding. Please enclose postage stamps with all communications hereafter.

Yours truly,   PRESS.

AN OWL CAME TO MY WINDOW ONE NIGHT AND HOOTED THREE TIMES.

GONE UNDER A CLOUD.

EVERY time I daguerreotype the life of Willie Castor I can not help feeling sorry for him. I am glad that I was born with a sympathetic nature so that my heart can go out to those who are unfortunate.

We are sometimes made unhappy by having too much money; again unhappiness may come to us through the transom of misfortune.

In the dark hours of the night we are sometimes awakened by the snarling of wolves at our doors.

We clamor to get into society and we clamor to get out.

The pursuit of happiness is a game of chasing forever and a day.

Willie Castor has tired himself out chasing celebrities, titles, society and happiness. Through not knowing how to go at it he has fallen all over himself and is now forced to hide under a cloud.

Willie differs materially from his grandpa. Away back in the smoky past Grandpa Castor lived on the banks of the Rhine in a little village not far from Heidelberg. At the age of three he had a presentiment that some day he would have money to throw at the ravens.

One day he shook his feet and a pair of wooden shoes hit the floor. He was preparing to leave home. He surrounded his feet with leather, said good-bye to the old folks and left for London. He remained in that city until the close of the American Revolution. In the autumn of 1783 he boarded a ship bound for America. The first thing he did after landing was to learn to skin coons. In a short time he was considered the champion coon-skinner of the country. He could catch more rabbits, mink, beaver, wild-cats and coons than any hunter of his time. This was the kind of society and happiness he was looking for and he found it.

Now I do not believe that Willie Castor would give two cents for all the coon skins in the country. He did not feel at home in the woods with a lot of varmints. Although he did not care for the hide business, he was ambitious nevertheless. At the age of thirty he got a notion into his head that his prominence was running down at the heel, so one day in an unguarded moment he pulled out his check book and bought himself a seat in the state senate.

He did not care for expenses while he was in politics. He could take a $30 bill and make it look like thirty cents in thirty minutes. Everybody had a drink with him while he was in the legislature, but the ventilation was bad there and he soon got out. He had a great many friends in New York at the time and they lasted as long as Willie was free with his money. These friends were ward barnacles and political bunions.

Later on Willie thought he would like to have a seat in Congress, but he foolishly left his check book at home and someone else got it. He was not to be outdone, however. He got on his ear one day and bought the post of minister to Italy.

He held that job down until a new president was elected. Then he received a note saying that on account of extenuating circumstances his pay would stop, so Willie returned to New York.

He did not like the freedom of the press, neither did he like to have people poke fun at him just because he had money, so he packed his trunk about ten years ago and moved to London where he can have people arrested for previousness and thereby gratify a three-ply yearning.

I am sorry he has had so many misunderstandings that could have been avoided. I am afraid his goose is cooked and his society sun has winked out. He should be possessed of some of his grandpa's coon-skin etiquette. He has certainly had a struggle to get in with the high muck-a-mucks of London.

Some time ago the Duchess of Boomski gave a candy pulling in honor of the Prince of Whalze. The list of guests was handed over to the Prince for inspection and the first thing he did was to give Willie Castor the blue pencil. When Willie heard about this it cut him dead.

Willie made a great mistake, too, when he wrote up his biography in a London magazine in which he claimed kin with Count Petro d'Castorgo of Castule. There is not a genealogist in the country who can not prove that this Spaniard in question never allowed either kraut or wienerwurst on his table. This is conclusive evidence that Willie is wrong, so the compilation of his genealogy was time lost. It were just as well he had been home that evening splitting kindling wood for morning.

When he invited the Prince of Whalze to take a 'possum dinner at his house he got his etiquette twisted and forgot to ask the Prince how he would like to be entertained, but told him that he would take him out black-berrying or else row him up the Thames in his new canoe. The Prince had been in the habit of naming his own pleasure, so he hinted to Willie that he would like a buggy ride. Willie tried to look as wise as a forest full of owls and he got as busy as a boy killing snakes hitching up his old gray mare to the buggy.

When Willie told Capt. Sir Artie Millet that he was not wanted at his house it was the straw that broke the backs of a whole herd of camels. Then to make matters worse he had the fact printed in the Morning Blister, so the whole town would know that he had given the captain the icy face. The captain felt hurt about the way Willie acted and I can not blame him.

I once read in a story paper where a boy's ma used to give him five cents every time he would take a dose of cod-liver oil. When he had saved up a dollar she would seize it and buy him another bottle. Now Willie would do well to save up a dollar and buy a book on royal etiquette.

The society of London is very different from that of my section of Arkansaw. If Willie and the captain were living down there they would have to settle their little difficulties with shotguns at ten paces. I understand Willie does not like the captain for the reason that when he met Willie's daughter he offered to hold her hand. To hold a girl's hand in Arkansaw is not considered any worse than eating pie with a spoon.

Willie made another move that did not prove a success. He sent a report to America that he was dead just to see what the people on this side would say. Some few believed it, but a majority of the people allowed the report was overdrawn. Now if he should have died accidentally before the report reached this country, he would have felt foolish.

When he declared that America was no place for a gentleman to live I thought perhaps he was joking, but I now understand that he did not make that remark, and he was not drinking at the time, either. Now that the Prince of Whalze has cut him out of royal society he will say the same thing about London. This is the reason I am sorry for him, because he has unfortunately cut himself out of society on both sides of the Atlantic. I do not know what will become of him now, unless he goes to South Africa and mixes up with Boer society. This is their busy season though, and they probably have little or no time for society. If I thought I was doing the square thing by him I would suggest that he go to China and get in with the Boxers. They are said to be the largest society in the world.

I do not think he will ever return to America, as he placed himself in a bad light here for leaving this country without working out his poll tax. He should have known at the time that he would get himself talked about. So all I can say for you, Willie, is this: When you have worried yourself half sick; when all the world looks gloomy; when December is as pleasant as May; when the flute or guitar are no longer strains of joy for your soul and when flowers look like thorns, then you just count a hundred and you will go to sleep.

SIGNS OF THE MOON.

HILE in Arkansaw I heard many farmers discussing the signs of the moon. This lead me to pry into the business, so that I might be able to talk knowingly on the subject. I have left no stone unturned in this study and I find that it is wise to be posted on the moon's action.

I also find by mathematical science that the moon is a $1 proposition. The first quarter I figure at 25 cents; the last quarter at the same price; and the half at 50 cents. This would make a full moon $1.

Some maniac gave the moon the wrong gender. She is a spasmodic drunkard, getting full as a goat ever so often. This in my mind is entirely out of place, as the fullness of the masculine gender does not look so disgraceful.

When potatoes are planted in the dark of the moon a large crop will be the result, providing there is a shortage of potato-bugs and grasshoppers. The ground must be well ploughed and the weeds kept down. Then if there is no drouth a large crop may be expected.

An old lady told me that she would not think of making soft soap in the dark of the moon, as it would be sure to boil over. I have never tried it, but I have

I FIND THAT IT IS WISE TO BE POSTED ON THE MOON'S ACTION.

thought if the fire was hot enough that soap would boil over in the light of the moon or even by candle light.

My mother told me when I was a boy that all children born in the dark of the moon would turn out to be trifling, and would fall into the habit of avoiding the truth. At that time I was old enough to worry and when she told me this worry set in on me like a San Francisco fog. I was anxious to know the condition of the moon the night I was born. I disliked to ask her as I was afraid she would say that I was born in the dark of the moon. Several weeks passed and my worry stuck to me like a wart on a spotted calf. One day when I thought she had forgotten what she had told me I asked her if the moon was light on the night I was born. She replied that only the stars were shining. That eased up my worry some, as I knew I would some day be a star, even though a trifling one. All this came back to me a short time ago when I was asked to assist in an entertainment. The manager wanted to know how much time I would occupy. I told him anywhere from ten minutes to four days. He looked at me in a kind of a dazed way and said:

"Let's see, I beg your pardon, but what is your name again?"

I pointed it out to him on the programme and then he said:

"Oh, yes, yes, I have heard of you. You will please not talk over ten minutes."

I knew a man who was born in the light of the moon and he was far from being trifling. He was extremely careless, however, and had a habit of pointing his pistol in a playful way. It went off at times and in so doing he kept killing people until the number reached seven. The community thought there should be a stop to such

THE CORONER'S JURY DECIDED THAT HE CAME TO HIS DEATH FROM THE LACK OF AIR.

carelessness, so one night when the moon was sinking behind a papaw grove, he was hanged to the limb of a water elm tree. The coroner's jury decided that he came to his death from the lack of air, or that he hung on to the rope too long.

When a boy born in the light of the moon turns out like that man I am glad my mother told me that dark-of-the-moon children are trifling. I would rather be trifling than live in a country where the air is not in breathing order.

I believe in doing everything in the dark of the moon. I think it brings greater success.

I remember once when I was too young to strike drills or dig ditches I climbed to the top of a neighbor's rail fence to enjoy the moonlight. By some accident my foot slipped and I fell into a watermelon patch. It occurred to me that I was not in a rush and as time was hanging heavy on my hands I might as well sample a melon. My neighbor saw by the light of the moon what I was doing and invited his bulldog to take charge of me. Years after that father told about driving an iron wedge and a couple of gluts into the dog's mouth in order to release the basement of my pants.

Some people born in the light of the moon are very unfortunate. I know a woman sixty-one years old who had never seen a train of cars. She was determined to ride on one before she died. She left home in Arkansaw one night to visit her daughter up north. Unfortunately the train on which she took passage was wrecked and a number of persons were killed and injured. A working crew was soon at the scene digging out the dead and rescuing the dying. The night was black, starless and wild. The crew worked like mad men. Every one who was able to move a hand gave heroic aid.

BY SOME ACCIDENT MY FOOT SLIPPED AND I FELL INTO A WATER MELON PATCH.

256

When the work of rescuing the dead and wounded was almost completed one of the wreckers discovered the old lady from Arkansaw wedged in between two wheels. In an excited voice he said to her:

"Are you hurt?"

"No, sir," she replied, "I am not hurt. Why do you ask?"

"Why do I ask? Great heavens, woman! don't you know that half the people who were on the train are dead?"

"Dead! Why, what killed them?"

"Why the wreck, of course."

"What wreck do you mean?"

"Say, for God's sake, have you been asleep and just now woke up? There has been a horrible wreck. Don't you hear all these men, women and children weeping?"

"No, I have not been asleep at all; have been awake all the way, but this is the first time I ever traveled on the cars and I did not know this was what you called a wreck. I thought it was the way the train always stopped."

The moon has everything to do with vines that twine. All vines of this class turn to the right. The fact is, all nuts on bolts in wagons turn to the right. Everything turns to the right, except the handle of a feather duster. That turns to the left. The poison oak vine does not twine, but when a boy is affected with this poison, he is sure to scratch with the right hand, even though he may be left-handed.

If the wind blows from the west to-day it will surely blow from the north the next time, then from the east, then from the south, and so on. It always keeps turning to the right. This rule works all over the world except

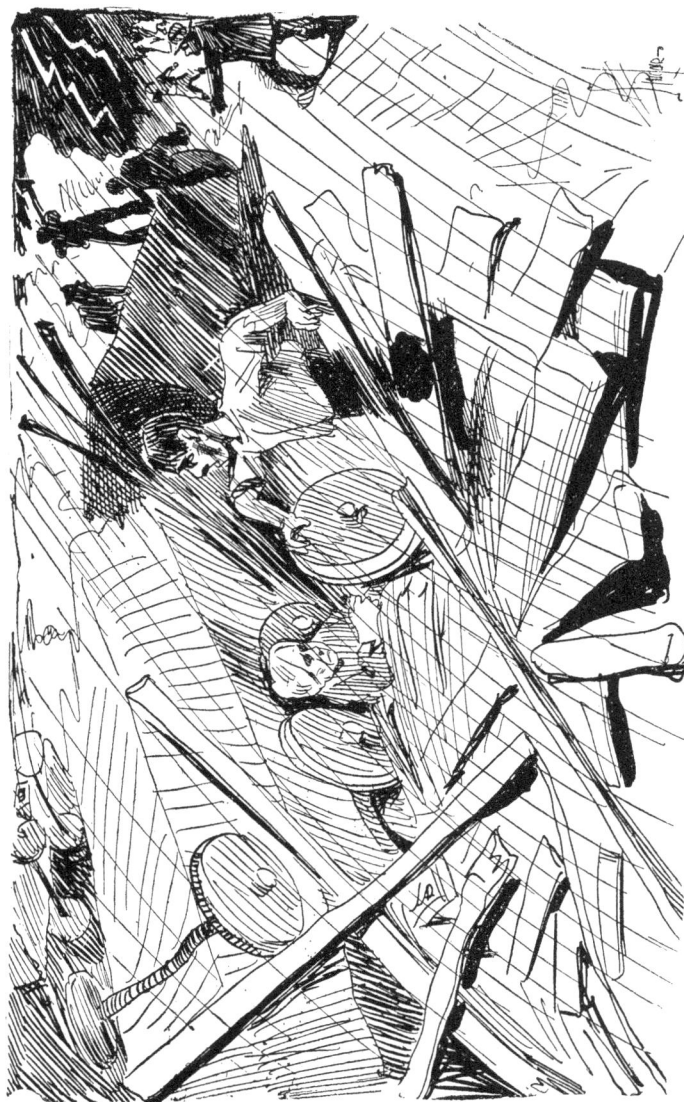

THE CREW WORKED LIKE MAD MEN. EVERY ONE WHO WAS ABLE TO MOVE A HAND GAVE HEROIC AID.

IT TOOK A PHYSICIAN FOUR DAYS TO PICK THE BIRDSHOT OUT OF THAT YOUNG MAN'S SYSTEM.

in Chicago. I have known the wind there to blow from five different directions at the same time.

A woman born in the light of the moon should be careful about committing marriage with a widower. A widower is a very peculiar man and is at any time liable to refer to the good qualities of his first wife. This is very painful to a second wife.

I heard a preacher say to his flock:

"If there is a man or woman in this congregation who knows of a perfect person on this earth I would be pleased to have them stand up." A lady seated pretty well back arose to her feet.

"I notice but one person standing," said the divine. "My good sister, do you know of a perfect person on this earth?"

"I knew of one, the only one I ever heard of," said the good sister.

"May I ask the name of that person?" inquired the minister.

"She is dead now. She was my husband's first wife."

Dark-of-the-moon children should never be baptized and vaccinated at the same time. I tried it myself and the baptism did not take.

If a young man is engaged to be married and the girl's pa is opposed to the match the dark of the moon is the time to marry, although an elopement may be necessary. An acquaintance of mine in southern Indiana tried the eloping business in the light of the moon. The girl's pa could see how to follow, and the result was it took a physician four days to pick the birdshot out of that young man's system.

I once made up my mind to go into the Boston mountains in Arkansaw and take a photograph of a moonshine distillery. I took with me a team of horses, a

"SAY, STRANGERS! DON'T YO' RECKON THET YO'UR FISHIN' JIST ER LEETLE TOO HIGH UP TH' KREEK?"

buggy and a driver named Eb. If he had another name I never found it out. He was a good, faithful, steady man, but the biggest coward in the state.

We started on our journey in the light of the moon. My friends advised me not to make the trip, as more than a dozen United States revenue officers had gone before me in other days and failed to return. When within two miles of the distillery we stopped on the bank of a stream under the pretense that we were fishing.

It was not long until I discovered a man on the opposite bank, who stood about six feet and nine inches high. He was about as slim as the country ever produced. He had on his shoulder a squirrel rifle, which looked to be as long as a fence rail. Eb said to me in a low voice:

"I'll bet dollars to coonskins that that feller is a moonshiner, and, if he should mistake us for 'revenuers,' I wouldn't give a gourd seed for our lives."

Eb was correct, as just then the long man across the stream yelled at us in a voice we could not fail to understand:

"Say, strangers! don't yo' reckon thet you're fishin' jist er leetle too high up th' kreek?"

"Why, I don't know, don't the fish bite here?" I replied.

"Wall, I've hearn tell thet they didn't. 'Sides thet, hit's er powerful unhealthy place fur strangers. I've knowed fellers ter come up hyar, an' git what they call bullet-patchin' fever; an' hit takes 'em away monstrous fast. Ef I wuz in you'ns place I'd jist fish erbout twenty miles furder down th' kreek. 'Course I haint no 'thority on fishin', but I know somethin' erbout er feller's health."

EB COULD ONLY KEEP IN SIGHT OF ME PART OF THE TIME.

I thanked him for his advice and then we moved. I have moved on other occasions in a hurry; but I can not recall the day when I made such good time as in getting away from that moonshiner. Eb had been bragging about how fast he could run the day before, but I did not imagine he was such a sincere mover; I have seen grayhounds in California do some pretty good running after jack rabbits, but they were slow compared with my rapid transit. Eb could only keep in sight of me part of the time, but as he said he knew the road I felt sure he would not get lost.

A moonshiner is not what one would call a Chesterfield. He does not care for an introduction. If a man is introduced by accident as we were, all that it is necessary for one to say is, "I am glad to meet you," then turn and break for home. This kind of moonshine etiquette seems to take the best, and is considered in good taste by all concerned.

It has so happened that all my troubles have taken place in the light of the moon. At the age of ten a neighbor gave me a pair of pants; although he had worn them a year or so before I got them, I thanked him kindly. He weighed about 240 pounds, while I tipped the scales at 116. They were very large pants for a boy of my size, but I did not mind that, as it did not take me long to cut the legs down. I would have also taken a reef or two in other sections of the garment had I known how.

The first time I wore them I found they were roomy enough to conceal a large-sized valise.

One night I went out 'possum hunting against pa's orders. When I returned he informed me he would settle with me next morning for not obeying him. Knowing full well what a good memory he had, I prepared

HE ALWAYS USED A LARGE SIZE HICKORY SWITCH.

for the settlement.   I took down that pair of adult pants and fixed them so the settlement would not sting.   I got hold of four grain sacks, sewed them together in the shape of a pillow, and then put it into the interior of the pants.

Morning came and pa was on hand.   He always used a large-sized hickory switch, and he was a very earnest man.   When he started in on the settlement I cried out with a loud voice, although I was suffering no pain. Every stroke sounded like a hired man beating a carpet during house-cleaning time.   Unfortunately for me pa discovered the patent attachment and invited me to take it off.   I obeyed and got as fine a taste of real old hickory as anyone ever experienced.

This happened in the light of the moon.

MY THIRD READER.

N LOOKING over my old third reader I find some short stories which are almost classical. Unless they are revised, however, I do not believe the up-to-date school-boy would enjoy them. The first story is about

THE CONTENTED MAN.

Once upon a time a poor hired man named Bob was going home after a hard day's work with a basket on his arm.

"What a fine layout I shall have when I reach home," said Bob with an upward inflection. "This piece of bay steer is well stewed, the garlic is nicely sliced, and the broth is well thickened with corn meal, so I have but to add a few dashes of red pepper and salt to make it good enough for a town marshal, and I have a dodger of hoecake at home, which will make a fine accompaniment to all this. How I long to get my feet under the table and get at that feed."

At this juncture he heard a racket at the roadside. Looking up he saw a red calf run up a tree and crawl into a hole.

"Ha, ha," said Bob, "what a fine present a nest of young calves would be for my sick neighbor who is down in bed with a pair of chilblains. I will make a sneak

267

LOOKING UP HE SAW A RED CALF RUN UP A TREE AND CRAWL INTO A HOLE.

up that tree and see if I can twist out a mess of these sly animals." So he dropped his basket and climbed up the tree. When about halfway up, with his fingers and toes sticking into the bark, he looked around and what did he see? An adult horse with his nose in the basket, trying to get the piece of steer. Bob did not take time to come down the tree in a dignified manner, but simply let go and fell. He did not want to lose time. The horse, however, was too swift for him, and he ran off with part of the contents of the basket.

"Well, well, well," said Bob, "wouldn't that frost you? Now I must be contented with plain, common, every-day soup. That, however, is not bad to take."

Bob walked up the road until he came to a tavern, where he saw a chum loafing on the front porch. Bob put his basket down and took a seat by his side. A pet mule which had been raised in the tavern came up slyly behind him and taking the bag of meal ran away with it to the shade of an old oak tree where it devoured it. Bob did not know that he had been touched until he had gone some distance on his way. He returned to the tavern, but too late, as the pet mule had gotten in its work.

"Well!" said Bob; "if these animals keep this up they will put me on the bum. The way things look now I cannot see anything but thin soup. Oh, well, I will boil a slice of bread with it and that will help some, anyway."

He journeyed on until he came to a babbling brook spanned by a foot-log. A girl with a fine supply of pimples was crossing the log from the other side. Bob, like a foolish man kept going and they met about half way and tried to pass. He wanted to be polite and give the poor girl the best of it. She in turn made

HE LEANED OVER ON THE AIR TOO FAR, AND WHEN HE STRUCK THE STREAM HE WENT DOWN ABOUT FORTY FEET.

goo-goo eyes at him and he lost his head. He leaned over on the air too far, and when he struck the stream he went down about forty feet. Fortunately he came up head first and therefore rescued himself from a watery grave. When he had coughed up a gallon or so of water he grabbed his basket and swam ashore. He then discovered that the salt had melted and the pepper had floated away. All he had left now was his garlic. When Bob got his wind he said:

"Well! well! wouldn't that make you sick? All I have to chew on tonight is bread and garlic. Last night I hadn't anything but bread. To-morrow night, if I don't get something more to eat I will have a fit." And he went on his way singing as before.

The next story of importance is about

THE HONEST MAN.

A granger one day called upon a neighbor who had money in the bank and who was also very fond of hunting. The granger complained that his wheat had been so mashed down and cut up by his neighbor's dogs that he believed that in some parts of his upper forty there would not be more than half a crop, and that he was there for the purpose of making a kick about it.

"Well, my granger friend," said the man with the money, "if you will give me an adequate conception of the damage my dogs have done to your wheat I will be glad to 'come to the front' with the stuff."

"With the help of a friend of mine," said the granger, "I have made an estimate, and I think an hundred plunks will make me easy. Now if you can jolly yourself a little and give me a check for an hundred I'll be much obliged to you."

"NOW I WANT TO RETURN THAT HUNDRED DOLLARS AND ADD FIVE HUNDRED."

The hunter gave him a check for the amount and the granger went direct to the village and got it cashed.

When the time for harvesting came the granger found that the crop on the upper forty was by far the best on the place. After the harvest he got a kink in his conscience, so he went back to the hunter and apologetically said:

"Do you recollect about that hundred you paid me?"

"Oh, yes; I remember it quite well; what about it?"

"Well, I will tell you. I find after threshing the part of the field your dogs mashed down the wheat turned out great. Actually it ran fifty bushels to the acre and beats anything I ever saw. Now I want to return that hundred dollars and add five hundred dollars to it just to show you that I am a good fellow."

When the granger had finished the hunter dropped dead.

SPELLBINDING.

OMETIMES I feel I want to un-buckle the throat-latch of my imag-ination and lengthen the trace-chains, so I can have elbow room and tell a story that really hap-pened.

When ·I was a shoeless boy my father told me he could see, by the way I worked, that I would some day be a political speaker, and that thousands of people would listen to my voice. I may say that the prophecy came true. Thousands of people have come to hear me talk, but they never remained until I had finished.

During last September I was invited to take the stump for the Republican party in the presidential cam-paign. Of course I might have taken the stump for the Democratic party, as I am a duplex speaker. I can make the same speech go both ways, by scratching out a few indefinite articles and perhaps throwing in a few adjec-tives here and there. I have no defined policy during a presidential campaign until I receive my mail.

The chairman of the bureau of speakers at the Repub-lican national headquarters in Chicago, invited me into his office for the purpose of testing me on political

"WHAT DID I UNDERSTAND YOU TO SAY YOUR FULL NAME WAS?"

science, and to sound me on my qualifications as a spell-binder. The following conversation took place:

"What did I understand you to say your full name was?"

"My full name is Honorable Press Woodruff."

"May I ask where you secured the appellation of Honorable?"

"Oh, I simply took that title, like all spellbinders take it, because there is no tax or restriction on such a handle."

"Where did you say you hailed from?"

"I hailed from Peaceful Valley, in the northwestern corner of Arkansaw, Washington county, forty miles from the Missouri line on the main traveled road to Pigram's mill near Nubbin Ridge in Turkey Hollow precinct four miles from Mount Zion schoolhouse."

"How is it that you are a Republican? Arkansaw is almost entirely Democratic."

"Well, you see, I flopped yesterday."

"What did you follow in Arkansaw?"

"I followed a plough most of the time."

"I mean, what was your calling?"

"Calling razor backs."

"I guess you do not quite understand me. I mean what was your profession."

"Catching driftwood is about the only business of which I have a technical and theoretical knowledge."

"Anything else?"

"Yes, I have been called a humorist."

"Do you find much fun in that business?"

"No, sir, very little."

"Why not? A humorist should be an embodiment of mirth and joy."

"Far from it, Mr. Chairman. A man who advertises himself as a humorist had better get funny the moment he walks out on the stage or some one is liable to cripple him for life."

"Besides being a driftwood catcher and a humorist, is there any other offense?"

"Yes, some others I could tell, but I prefer to keep them quiet."

"Well, I guess you will do, as you certainly have an unreasonable contempt for danger."

"Yes, I dare say I have that. I have had everything else, from a pink-tinted boil to spavin in the head."

"You may take the stump, as I believe you have all the qualifications of a spellbinder; but you must not talk politics, as the Republican party is in this campaign to win, and there must be no mistakes. I will send you along with the Honorable J. C. Kemp, of Ohio. You will be the humorist of the combination; in other words, you will be a comedy prologue to a serious drama. At each meeting you will open up with a funny talk so as to get the audience in a jolly mood, then the Hon. Kemp will follow you and discuss the issues of the day."

The chairman then called into his office an emaciated biped of the genus homo. He was comely, but not arrogant; he was psychological, but not assuming. His address was indigenous to the soil of Ohio. In deportment he stood ninety-eight. In civil government he stood one hundred and one. At the table he could stand for everything except cornmeal mush.

We left Chicago for Grand Forks, North Dakota, with instructions to work under the auspices of the chairman of the state central committee. Hon. Kemp is a very reticent, conservative, matter-of-fact gentleman, and humor to him is pathetic, so he looked forward to my first appearance with sadness. He told me on the quiet he thought I ought to talk politics right from the jump.

I told him I would leave that entirely to his wise judgment.   He instructed me to go to the town of Wahpeton on the night of October 3 and address a big meeting, while he would go to Fairmount and make a speech.   In due time I boarded a train for Wahpeton, where the eager voters were waiting for a good thing.   The conductor and brakeman looked at me suspiciously as I occupied two seats, but they never suspected I was a humorist.   I overheard the conductor say to the brakeman: "That guy looks like a spotter."

As that train rushed madly through the land of windmills and blizzards I looked out of the window across the great expanse and fell into a deep reverie.   Before leaving Chicago I had promised the Venus of my heart, the sunshine of my existence, and a gleam of loveliness and joy, that I would not discuss the political issues from a Republican standpoint.   She was born under the bright rays of a southern sun and knew no political creed except that of Jefferson Davis.   I had given her the key to the front door of my heart and told her that the lock was love and no one could enter there.   I knew full well what I was about to do—break my promise.   I tried to dismiss the thought from my mind, but in vain. We had named a day when we were to attend a hymeneal feast.   What must I do?   Many times I asked myself this question as I sat there 'twixt love and duty.

But little did I know of the trouble which awaited me in Wahpeton.   When the train rolled into the station a committee rushed up and asked me if I was the speaker.   I replied that I was.   With all honors due a spellbinder I was loaded into a carriage and driven away to the opera house.   The band played "Stars and Stripes Forever," the throng toted torchlights, a thousand tin horns rang out on the chilly night and dogs of all breeds coughed up their saddest wails. In calling the multitude to order the chairman said:

"Ladies and Gentlemen. (Applause.) I now have the very great pleasure of introducing to you one of the greatest political speakers that ever made tracks in North Dakota mud. (Sickening applause.) He is a son of old Ireland and—(deafening cheers)—every time he opens his mouth he says something. (Great applause and cries of 'louder!') He knows Bobbie Burns by heart and could recite Robert Emmet's speech at the early age of four. He is a man of strong character and a lover of liberty. (Roar of applauses and cries of 'Down in front!') In his address to-night I ask you to give him your earnest attention, as he is able to present facts and statements over which you can ponder deliberately. If your foresight is as good as your retrospection, my friends, you will certainly know how to vote on the sixth of November. (Yells of 'Good boy!' from the audience.) Do not allow your prejudice to run away with your judgment, but respect and value your vote the same as you would one of your family. An honest man is the grace of his country. We want honest men in office. Now, ladies and gentlemen, I will present to you the speaker of the evening, the Honorable J. H. O'Riley."

It was some little time before the applause died away. The greeting was most gratifying, but I was puzzled as I knew that my name was not O'Riley and I also knew that I was not Irish. However, I was filled up to the æsophagus with Republican doctrine and I sailed into that audience like a Webster. I talked prosperity about five minutes and I noticed the audience began to look wicked and nervous. I brought my favorite gesticulations into action and fired thirteen-inch capsules of sound money doctrine right and left. It was not long until some one let out a frightful yell:

"Say, you big lobster, go crawl under the floor."

This was followed up by a number of cat calls, and "tell the guy to sit down." I could not see for the life of me what I had said that would offend any one, as I was doing my best. I continued for a few minutes longer, during which time I spoke harshly of W. J. Bryan's insincerity. Then came a cry from the audience: "Throw the piano at that big chromo."

I saw in a moment that that audience wanted something else besides prosperity doctrine. So I started in to give them a dose of fiat money. In part I said:

"Gentlemen, you can not place silver on a parity with gold, no more than you can lift the latch of Eden's gate, or legislate that a rabbit's hide shall sell for the same price as a beaver's skin."

Then a dozen voices all yelled at once: "Set the dogs on 'im." "Put him out." "What's that dub's name? I'll bet he is so crooked that his blood won't circulate." "Ah, go home and throw mud at yourself." "Come off the perch; yo've got hornets in your bonnet." And a hundred other jeers at the same time. I saw that consternation was inevitable. By the next ten seconds everything was coming my way. The local celebrities all left the stage for safety. I stood there almost transfixed. I did not know what to do; and there was no use to try to say another word, as no one could hear me. While the air was full of stove wood, chair legs and pants buttons, the chairman rushed up to me and excitedly said: "Say, Mr. Speaker, ain't your name O'Riley?"

"No, sir," I said, "my name is Woodruff and I was sent here to make a Republican speech."

GENTLEMEN, YOU CANNOT PLACE SILVER ON A PARITY WITH GOLD NO MORE THAN YOU CAN LIFT THE
LATCH OF EDEN'S GATE.

Then in a fit of rage he said: "Well, by gosh, you had better get to the devil for this is a Democratic meeting."

I did not run or walk out the back way, but just fell out as I knew I would be sure of making my escape.

I then found my way to the Republican meeting and the committee had about given up my coming. I asked the chairman why in the name of common sense he or the reception committee did not meet me at the station.

"Well," he said, "I was at the station to meet you, and I saw you get off the train, but as you did not look to me like a stump speaker I made up my mind you was either a grave-stone agent or a barn-stormer."

When I returned to Grand Forks Mr. Kemp asked me what kind of a meeting I had in Wahpeton. I told him two kinds.

North Dakota rolled up a great majority for the Republican party. I have learned since then that if I had been kept out of the state the majority would have been much larger.

The chairman of the bureau of speakers found out by some means that I was dropping my humor and talking politics. He wired me to stick to my mirth, as the Republican party did not care to take any chances.

We were then ordered to the state of Minnesota and my first day's experience in that state was a sad one. While traveling on a fast mail between Morehead and St. Paul I noticed a thrashing crew at work in a field near the railroad and I pulled the bellcord to stop the train. The conductor's hair turned red in less than one minute. He demanded of me with a voice like a sea-dog to explain why I stopped the train. I told him I simply wanted to get off and take a straw vote. The conductor cooled down to about ten below freezing and told me to go ahead but to make haste. Somehow or other he changed his mind while I was taking the straw vote and pulled out and left me. I did not lose my temper. I talked that crew into calling together all the farmers in the neighborhood that night, so I could give them a political dessertation. I made a speech in a stable, and heard one man say: "Well, that's a horse on me."

The next day I was able to get a train into St. Paul and again join my serious drama.

We were dispatched hither and yon by the chairman of the State Central committee. When we arrived at Winona I heard the hotel clerk say to the bus driver:

"Bill, who all did you haul up?"

His reply was: "There was one gentleman and a humorist."

On the sixth day of November the Hon. Kemp returned to Chicago. On the sixteenth of that month the chairman of the bureau of speakers made some inquiries as to my whereabouts, as I had not reported at headquarters.

No one seemed to know anything about me. The committee advertised in the St. Paul papers and I was discovered in southern Minnesota still talking for the Republican party, ten days after the election. The committee wired me as follows:

"Come home; the show is over and McKinley is elected."

In due time I found myself in the Windy City. I reported at headquarters and the chairman with all the rest extended the glad hand and gave me a welcome which I shall always appreciate.

During all these weeks I had been in the campaign I had never received a missive from the one to whom

I had promised to be faithful. Had she heard of my political work or was it possible that my mail had not been forwarded? I carefully weighed all this in my mind before I could decide upon the proper course to pursue. I could not think of losing her, as my hopes would be forever blasted. Could that true heart of hers have grown cold? Would she again meet me at the garden gate, overlook my broken promise, and greet me with that pair of loving eyes which so oft had thrilled my very soul? These and other thoughts rushed through my weary brain and stabbed deeply my sin-sick soul. I called a carriage, resolved to go to her home and tell her all. My heart was heavy, but I was determined to know my fate within an hour. I rang the door bell and the servant was soon in possession of my card. My little angel's dear old father greeted me kindly. After a brief chat about my trip in the west he asked:

"Well, I reckon you heard about the girl, didn't you?"

"No, sir, I have had no news from her whatever."

"Why, do you mean to tell me that you haven't heard anything about her?"

"You have my word of honor, sir, I have never heard one word about her since I left here last September."

"Well, I suppose you remember you made her a promise when you went away?

"Yes, sir, I remember it quite well."

"Well, she heard about your speeches in North Dakota, and I am sorry to say that you had just as well try to work a pair of jay-birds to a dray as to attempt to win her hand now."

"Pray, sir, may I ask why?"

"Why, simply because she has married a Democrat, and moved to the Sunny South.

A TRIP TO GOOSE CREEK.

INCE I began writing this book, which was on the second Tuesday of last Spring, I have waited for a few characters to be hanged or shot, so I could tell about how it happened. Up to this hour, however, they are still living and enjoying good health.

Last month I made up my mind to take a trip to Arkansas and look over the ground for the purpose of noting what changes had taken place in twenty-six years three months and thirteen days. When I arrived in Fayetteville I noticed the State University had made a big improvement in the town. I went to this tower of learning and asked one of the teachers if he would let out school a short time in honor of my arrival, so the school children could get a chance to see me. He asked me for my name, and I promptly told him. Then he aid:

"Now, if you come pestering around here again, I have a couple of bull-dogs, which I will let out in your honor, if it is any favor to you."

This was the first great change that came to my notice. In my school days the teacher would let out school for a dog fight or a case of measles. Things, however, are different in the educational line since the passing of McGuffey's reader and Webster's blue-black elementary spelling book. School boys of to-day dress in uniforms and chew flat tobacco. They do not have to go home on Saturday and help their hump-back fathers split rails and set out cabbage plants. About all the exercise they get is making their own pulmonary cigarettes. In my day, when a boy was bad the teacher sent him out into the woods for a yearling club with knots on it, and a settlement was soon fixed up between them. To-day a school boy is punished in a very different manner. If he is hard to manage, the teacher allows him a vacation of from one week to three months for reflecting purposes.

The first day in Fayetteville I met my old teacher of Double Springs, the one who punished me for sticking my big toe in the crack of the floor. I swore at the time if ever I grew up to be a man that I would give him a first-class thrashing. After I talked to him a few moments I learned that he had been teaching athletics for eighteen years. He weighed 198 pounds and wore number eleven shoes without socks. He told me his toe nails grew so long he had to chop them off with an ax. He also told me that he had a standing challenge at his school to knock out any four of his students at one time in a friendly bout. I changed the subject, and after we had talked a few minutes about Arkansaw climate I got away under the pretext of visiting friends.

The next day I met a man who knew me when I was a young sapling. He said:

"Do you see that old man standing on the corner with his right leg missing?"

"I do," I said.

"DO YOU SEE THAT OLD MAN STANDING ON THE CORNER WITH
HIS RIGHT LEG MISSING?"

"Well, sir, that is old Uncle Bill Holden; I reckon you recollect him, don't you?"

"I certainly do; he lived right south of our place on the day the battle of Pea Ridge was fought."

"Well, I was going to tell you: he was one hundred and three years old just a little while before Christmas. He does not look as spry as he did a year ago by any means. He lost his leg in the battle of Prairie Grove, during the civil war, and he has been in hard luck ever since. He has been afflicted with consumption for the last ten years, and, besides, he lost the use of his left arm. About two years ago he had the smallpox, and three months later he was in the hospital flat on his back with typhoid pneumonia, and that almost took him away. He would perhaps have gotten along very well, but his last illness left him subject to hard fits, and they are so severe that he seems weakened from the effects. As soon as he was able to get up and about he was kicked by a horse, and that gave him a backset. For all that, the doctors say, if he would leave off the use of snuff, he might live several years longer."

"His misfortunes and infirmities have certainly made great changes in him since I left here, but then, of course, his age is against him."

"No, I think not. You see, in Arkansaw they live to be very old. Only a short time ago I heard Uncle Thad Miner say that he expected to live until the judgment day, and even then some one would have to take an ax to him before he would quit the earth. Yes sir-ee, they do certainly grow very old in Arkansaw. Why, I recollect that when the 'Frisco' road came into this place, old Grandpa Peter Lampkins, who was at that time 111 years old, walked into town, a distance of seventeen miles, with a middling of meat on his shoulder to see his first train, and didn't think anything of it. It is the climate and soil. The latter is so rich that we can raise anything from a soap-gourd to the biggest kind of a fuss without irrigating."

"Excuse me for interrupting you, but who is that old gentleman standing there in front of the hotel?"

"Why, that's old Uncle Nick Diller. He is known here as the village story teller. He has been running that hotel for the last eighteen years. Oh, he is the life of the town, and besides he is a great hunter and fisherman, and, while I think of it, I must tell you a true story about him.

"Some time ago he went over on White river to catch a few dozen fish. He invited several traveling men to go along. They didn't have to be coaxed much, for you know a traveling man will go any place if there is any sport in it. Uncle Nick is a great hand for dogs, and he seldom goes fishing without a few with him. Some of them are thoroughbreds and some are just plain dogs— that is to say, yellow. On this occasion he took along one of the yellows, which he had been teaching to retrieve from puphood. He had this yellow well trained. The fact is, he named him Yellow. Every time he threw a stick, fence rail, a stick of cord wood, or even a wagon tongue, into a stream, Yellow would jump in and bring out the goods to his master. Well, on this day he took along a few sticks of giant powder in order to get plenty of fish with but little work and to give the traveling men an idea of how it was done. Well, sir, now here comes the killing part of it; I mean the joke. I think Uncle Nick was trying to show off a little that day, as all the drummers were guests at his hotel. He said to them: 'Now, I will take this stick of giant powder and throw it into the river. When it explodes you will see 17,964 fish come to the top, belly up. We will then jump into a skiff, row out and spend an hour in picking them up. I guess you fellows better get into the skiff so you can be ready to row out as soon as the explosion takes place.'

"The traveling men seated themselves in the skiff and waited for orders.

" 'Now, fellows, when I count three be ready,' said Uncle Nick. " 'Are you all in the skiff?'

" 'We are.'

" 'Then here goes.'

"At that he threw the stick of powder into the river, and the moment the dog saw it strike the water he plunged after it and grabbed it with his teeth. When Uncle Nick saw what Yellow was doing he had cold and hot flushes up his back. He realized that he could not coax the dog to drop the powder, so he made a rush for the woods. The louder he yelled at the dog to drop the stick the faster he went. Just as the dog was within thirty feet of him the powder exploded, and Uncle Nick fell to the ground in a dead faint. The drummers rushed up and worked with him for some time before they could bring him to life again. When he recovered consciousness he asked:

" 'Where is the dog?' The drummers did not know, as there was no sign of a dog about. After a close search, a piece of the dog's tail was found in the forks of a sapling. From that day to this, if any one speaks to Uncle Nick about retrievers, he simply refuses to talk."

"Well, now, that is all right about Uncle Nick and his retriever; but what interests me most now is a drive out west of here about six miles. I want to see what changes have taken place on Goose Creek and Soda Flat. I want to hang around a while out there where the sapsuckers and gray squirrels are the thickest. Can you direct me to some livery stable where I can get a team?"

"Can I?" said my friend, whose name was Jim Powers, by the way. "I cannot direct you to any place else, because I am running a stable myself. You just lean up against the court house there and rest yourself while I hitch up, and we will soon be on the way."

"Do you see that mound over yonder to the left?" said Jim as we drove along. "Well, sir, that is what they call Gallows Hill. Many years ago a young fellow was caught stealing sheep, besides that he killed a man one night, and, as you know, that was adding insult to injury, and carrying his devilment a little too far. The sheriff got after him, and told him that he would have to be more careful, or he would be compelled to let the law take its course. The young man didn't pay the least attention to the advice, but showed a vindictive spirit that made the sheriff angry, and he took the young fellow before the bar of justice; and the result was the judge sentenced him to be hanged until he was as dead as a mackerel. The funniest thing about the whole affair was the cold blooded way he acted on the gallows. The day for hanging him up was set, and the whole towns of Fayetteville, Farmington, 'Possum Trot and Goose Creek turned out to see the thing come off. I never saw such a multitude of people at one time. Yes, sir-ee, that was a crowd for your chin hemps and manila sprouts; all turned out.

"On the scaffold the sheriff asked him if he had anything to say before the sentence was executed.

" 'Yes, sir,' he said. 'I have a dying request to make. Take this bar of soap to the man from whom I took the sheep, and tell him to wash his neck. Tell him, also, that when his last day comes, he had better wear an asbestos suit. Sheep's wool won't do him any good there. Now, Mr. Sheriff, the trap you have set for this bird is, I hope, in good order; just throw the trigger.' The sheriff did as he was requested, then the bets were all off."

"Do they hang people very often around here nowadays?"

"No, not in this section. It is not the fad it once was. That kind of punishment has gone out of style. Speaking of hanging; do you see that little meeting house on the hill there? Well, that is Mount Nebo. There is where Aunt Tina Sampson professed religion long before the war. She was a mighty good woman, I tell you; but for all that, she died with a broken heart. She was the mother of seven boys, and every durned one of them turned out bad. It was a shame the way those boys carried on their mischief. Four of them were lynched for jayhawking during the war and the other three were shot for robbery. It was too bad, on Aunt Tina's account, but they had to go.

"Just a mile from here is where we had the awful cyclone a few years ago."

"Excuse me for interrupting you, Jim, but I did not know you had cyclones in Arkansaw."

"You didn't? Well, I should cough up a rabbit. And you never heard of an Arkansaw cyclone? Why, you must have been stuck away in some hollow log sound asleep all these years. We have a brand of cyclones down here different from any I ever read of. We have the regular down in front kind. The one I am going to tell you about was a twister. It was full of kinks. It had its tail twisted somewhere down on Beaver creek, and the closer it came this way the madder it got; and by the time it reached Sid Kain's barn it had turned green. Say, talk about pranks. It took all the mules and horses out

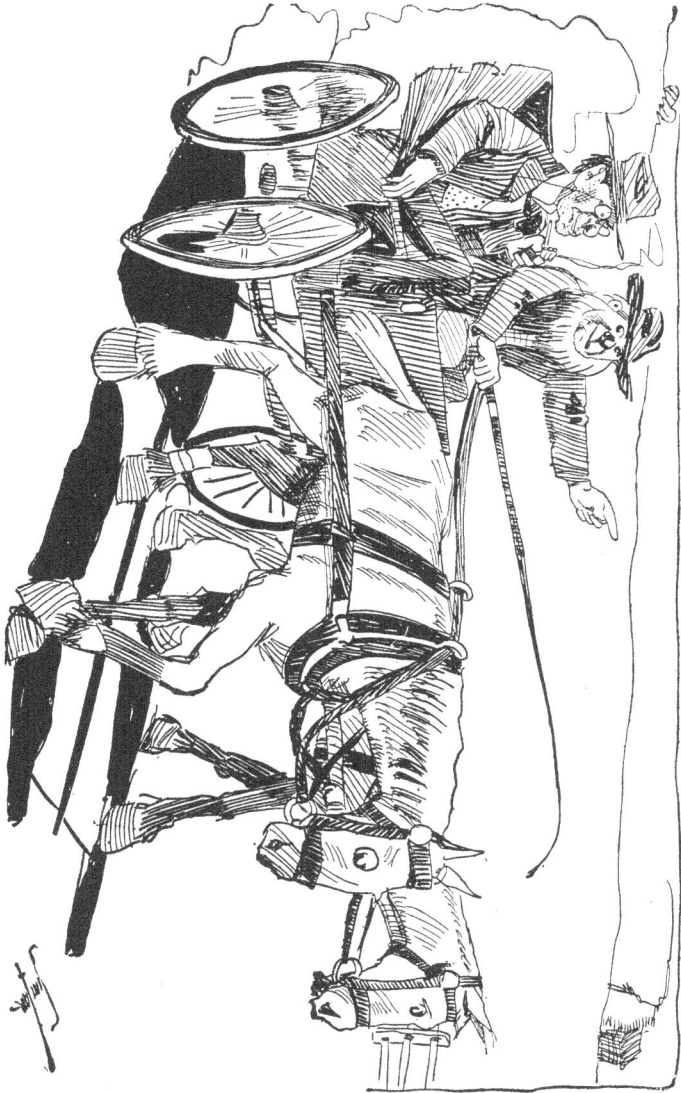

"THERE IS WHERE AUNT TINA SAMPSON PROFESSED RELIGION LONG BEORE THE WAR."

and tied them to trees; then it deposited the barn over twenty-five townships. Oh, it was a sure enough disgrace the way that thing acted. Just beyond the barn the Benton family lived, and that twister struck their house and set the whole family out into the middle of the county road, and not one of them was hurt The old lady was sticking in the mud up to her waist and

"SINGULAR AS IT MAY SEEM, NOT ONE OF THEIR CHICKENS WAS KILLED, BUT THEY WERE PICKED AS CLEAN AS IF BY HUMAN HANDS."

the old man's shoes were untied. The children were fastened together with a cotton rope. Their house has never been heard of since. Singular as it may seem, not one of their chickens was killed, but they were picked as clean as if by human hands. One old rooster escaped with just one tail feather. He was a sight, I tell you.

"The Benton family owned an organ, and I'll be blamed if that organ wasn't found sitting in one corner of a stable four miles from there, and it wasn't even out of tune. Yes, sir-ee, it was an awful cyclone. All Mr.

Benton had left with which to start in life again was that organ and a few dozen featherless chickens.

"That house over there in the woods is where old man Roletts used to live. No use talkin', he was a case. You know he never believed in education. When Mr. Hestler came to this section to get up a school he asked Roletts if he wanted to send any of his children. Roletts said he did not see the use, as schooling made a boy so smart he was trifling. He said he could take his oldest boys and lock them up in a barn and they could make five dollars a day swapping old clothes with each other. Yes, sir, he lived to the age of sixty and never learned to read or write. They told some great stories on the old fellow, but for all that he was the best judge of a coon dog in the whole county.

"He once subscribed for a weekly paper, and he had to take it over to Lige Powers and get him to read it. In one issue there was a lengthy article advising the Arkansaw farmers to plant plenty of corn, as there would be a great many immigrants come in that fall. 'Hold on thar, Lige,' said Roletts, 'don't read so durned fast. Now, what in th' jumped-up-gee-whilicans is 'n immigrant?'

"'Blamed if I know,' said Lige, 'unless it's something kind of between a coon and a ground hog, because I know that ground hogs are hell on corn.'"

We drove over to my old home on Goose Creek. There had been many changes. A woman was making soap out by the ash-hopper. The soap-kettle looked natural, but the ash-hopper did not. It was sickening to see how that ash-hopper had been allowed to go to rack. The spring house had been washed away one night, and had stayed away. I asked one of the men there what he raised on the farm these days.

"About the same as you see around here," he said; "rag-weeds, turnips, yellow dock, boils, poison oak, and

some ague; that is about all. When the distemper, cholera and blind staggers are not bad we can raise a pretty
fair crop of hogs. When we bought the farm from you
folks we thought there was some soil on it. We didn't
know, or even stop to think, that any man would fence in
eighty acres of flint rocks and then call it a farm. Of
course, that hillside land is pretty good, but it is so
steep that we have to tie the pumpkin vines to a tree.
The first year we took the place we did not think of that.
One night there was a storm, and a thousand pumpkins
rolled off that hill into Goose Creek and washed away.
The creek was high, and the last we heard of the pumpkins they had reached the Illinois River, going faster
than ever."

I took a farewell look at the old place, then went back
to town.

"ONE NIGHT THERE WAS A STORM, AND A THOUSAND PUMPKINS ROLLED OFF THAT HILL INTO GOOSE CREEK."

CUPID AND PSYCHE.

HERE once lived a king whose crown was seven and three-quarters, while his right size was six and one-eighth. This crown came down over his ears, and it made him look very blase. His wife was a queen, of course, but she did not monkey around the throne very much. She had all she could do to take care of the chickens and entertain company. They had three grown-up daughters. The oldest two were simply dreams; and the people around often stopped plowing corn and took a week off just to get a look at these killing soubrettes. The beauty of the youngest could not be expressed in dialect. The language of the finest word painter that ever dipped a quill would be poverty-stricken when it comes to describing this fairy's beauty. People drove a great distance up the pike to get a look at her. They feasted their eyes and paid her a homage that made Venus wild with jealousy. Her name was Psyche, and, unfortunately, she was only mortal; while Venus was immortal, and very sore on Psyche. We cannot very well blame Venus for being jealous; for when the truth is known, Venus at that time could give the whole world cards and spades on being a fine looker,

No beauty, mortal or immortal, could hold a candle to her.

When Psyche, the young virgin, passed along the streets the men sang her praises in rag time and threw twenty-dollar bunches of carnations and lilacs in her path.

This perversion of homage to Psyche, which belonged only to the gods and goddesses, caused Venus to turn up her nose. The very sight of Psyche gave her hot and cold flushes so she ran her fingers through her ambrosial locks and in an angry moment she said to herself: "Am I, the whole thing as I am, the official beauty of all the goddesses, to be outdone by this cross-eyed, dough-faced, round - shouldered, pigeon - toed, sap - headed mortal Psyche? No, no, not with me she don't. I guess I know my business. I will allow no one to take charge of the beauty department but myself. Did not the sheep herder, whose judgment was approved by Jove himself, hand me the palm of beauty which was head and shoulders over my rivals, Pallas and Juno? If I know myself, Psyche will not take my honors from me. I will yet make her glad to ask my forgiveness, and if she does not, I'll sure enough put her on the run."

She thought the matter all over, and figured on how she could get even with Psyche for being so beautiful and attractive. She called her son Cupid into the front room for consultation. Cupid had wings and carried a bow and arrow. Besides being a high-class love maker, he was a regular cut-up. When it came to lady-killing he was there with the goods. As a flirt he was a record breaker. So Venus said to him:

"My son, I want you to get your wings in good flying shape, take a trip down to the earth, and get square with that contumacious Psyche for my sake. Give your mother a chance to get a hatful of sweet revenge, for she needs it

SHE CALLED HER SON CUPID INTO THE FRONT ROOM FOR CONSULTATION.

300

in her business. Infuse into her heaving breast a fearful desire to marry some ragged, can-rushing, low-down tramp, so that afterwards she will have a chance to reap a big crop of mortification."

Cupid got foxy under his mother's guidance, and put up the following job:

In his mother's back yard, near the smokehouse, there were two fountains. One was filled with syrup and the other with fluid extract of gall. Cupid filled two quart bottles, one from each fountain. He tied them to his quiver and struck out for Psyche's domain. She had been to a dance the night before, and when he found her she was dead to the world. She was sleeping like an anaconda during its lethargic season. He shed a few drops from his gall fountain over her lips; though the very look of that fair face almost moved him to pity. Then to assure himself that she would wake up he touched her in the side with the tip end of his arrow. At the touch her eyes flew open, and Cupid was by her side, but invisible. He was so excited that in flitting around he accidentally wounded himself with his own arrow. He cared little about the wound, but was anxious to make some repairs on the mischief he had played with Psyche, so he poured the contents of the bottle of syrup on her hair to counteract the effects of the gall.

Psyche, with all her charms and good looks, had never derived any benefit from them. Venus had been making snoots at her, and all told, things were going wrong, so what could the poor girl do? It is true, every one was rubbering at her with admiration, and spoke well of her, and all that; but neither king, dude, plebian horse trainer nor tavern keeper ever made a break and offered to take her in out of the wet and marry her. The two sisters I have already mentioned had not been married a great while.   They were tied up to a couple of pale-faced royal princes, but both, unfortunately, were unhappy.

Dear reader, have you ever made a study of a royal prince?   Allow me to give you the definition of a royal prince when he is at his best.   In zoological science he is called a parody on an accident.   He is a door knob upon which an old hen has sat but failed to hatch.   Can you blame these two sisters for not being happy?

Psyche was housed up in her lonely apartments dead tired of her solitude and sick of her beauty.   Of course her make-up called for lots of flattery, but she had failed to awaken any kind of love.   Her father and mother, fearing that they were in some kind of a mix-up with the gods, went over to the oracle Apollo for a consultation.   His answer was:

"It is destined that Psyche will fall in love with some mortal and become his wife.   Her future husband is at the top of a lofty mountain.   He is a monster with large burnt-umber eyes and mattress hair whiskers.   His hair is a sea green, and neither men nor gods can handle him."

Now, this awful decree of the oracle put the whole neighborhood to thinking, and Psyche's parents went out and got full up to the neck on grief.   Then Psyche said to them:

"Why do you take on about me?   You should have done the grieving act when all the men showered honors on me and when they threw tube roses and pansies at me and at the same time called me a Venus.   That was the time you should have done your weeping.   I know that as long as I am mortal Venus will be my hoodoo and I will have plenty of trouble on her account.   But never mind, here I am, and I submit; so lead me to the top of the mountain."

"42 IS A MONSTER WITH LARGE BURNT-UMBER EYES AND MATTRESS HAIR WHISKERS."

In due time everything was prepared for the trip. The royal maid got into the procession like a hired girl, and the people strung out like a grand march at a country dance. It looked more like a funeral, however, than it did a bride-elect going to meet her future. Her parents were shedding tears as large as osage oranges. It seemed like such a disgrace to see poor Psyche marched up the mountain to marry some monster to whom she had never been introduced.

When the summit was reached Psyche was left alone. The procession returned home in single file.

While Psyche stood on the top of the mountain, breathing heavily from the long walk, and with her mellow eyes soaked in tears, a kind and gentle zephyr lifted her quietly into the air and took her away to a dale of flowers. There she laid herself down and fell into a peaceful sleep. When she awoke she looked about, and before her was a beautiful grove. She found her way into the midst of it and discovered a fountain. It was not hydrant water, but pure and crystal. Near by stood a magnificent palace that would suit any kind of a woman —the kind of palace poets write about. Psyche knew at a glance that it was not put up by mortal hands, but was erected to order for some god's summer resort. She was, like all women, very curious, so she ventured to look around for awhile. She glanced first to the left and then to the right, and everything filled her soul with amazement and pleasure. Pillars of gold supported the roof, and the walls were set with diamonds, sapphires, rubies and onyx. While she was so busy looking at the wonderful paintings she heard a voice, which said:

"Fair lady, we are your servants and at your command. You cannot see us, but we are here to treat you right. We are the only invisible servants you ever had, and you can never discharge us. Now, go to your

A KIND AND GENTLE ZEPHYR LIFTED HER QUIETLY INTO THE AIR
AND TOOK HER AWAY TO A DALE OF FLOWERS.

chamber and take a rest; then you can take a bath and get ready for a supper that will be heavenly."

Psyche did as they commanded, and when she had rested and bathed she repaired to the dining-room and put her feet under the mahogany. There she enjoyed herself as never before. The music by the Aeolian invisible string band was certainly entrancing.

All this was very good, and Psyche enjoyed it for a time; but she wanted a chance to see her husband. He had a habit of coming home after dark and skipping out before daylight. He was full of love and a most exemplary man, but Psyche was crazy to see what he looked like. Many times she would ask him to remain until daylight so she could get a chance to size him up, but he always refused for reasons best known to himself. This quieted Psyche for a short time, but at length she grew impatient at living alone in the palace with no one to talk to but invisible servants and a pair of house cats.

At last she grew homesick, and wanted to have her two sisters pay her a visit. One night when Cupid came home she asked him if he would care much if her sisters paid her a visit. He reluctantly gave his consent. So she sent word for the sisters to come on. They climbed the mountain and worked Zephyr for a couple of ærial passes down into the valley where Psyche lived. She was tickled almost to death to see them, and she surely made the wives of the royal princes feel at home in her grand palace. The two sisters had never seen anything so splendid, and they at once proceeded to get jealous of her good luck. So they sought to create a disturbance. They burdened her with a lot of questions, many of which she did not answer directly. They made her admit that she had never seen her husband, and that he came home at night and went away before the break of day.

Then the sisters stuffed her head full of dark suspicion.

"Do you recollect," they said, "about the Pythian oracle that said you would marry some terrible monster? How do you know but what you are sleeping with a snake a hundred feet long? It may be that he will be good to you for awhile, then, in a fit of madness, get in some night and eat you up. Now, you had better take our advice, and find out what kind of a fanged reptile you are rooming with. Get yourself a razor and make it sharp. Then get a tallow candle and hide it, with the razor, under the bed, so he will not see them. When he comes home, wait until he is sound asleep; then climb out of bed, light the candle, and, whatever you do, don't forget your razor. Take the candle in one hand and the razor in the other; and if you find out that he is a snake, why, don't hesitate to cut his head off; then you will have your liberty, and you can go home and have a big time with us girls, as you used to."

Little did Psyche dream her own sisters were putting up a job on her. She secured the razor and candle as they advised and waited for the coming of her nocturnal husband. In due time her better half entered the palace through some crack and crawled into bed. When he fell asleep and began snoring a tune that sounded like a dry goods clerk tearing off seven yards of bed-ticking, she slipped out of bed, struck a match on her center table, and proceeded to take the first peep at her husband. She did not discover a poisonous monster, with ten-inch fangs, as she had expected, but the most charming of all immortals. There he rested in his pink silk pajamas, with his golden hair spread out all over the pillow. He had on a pair of wings, covered with dew, which was collected while flying through the night. His cheeks were crimson, and his neck was whiter than frost. As she leaned over him to get a good view of his heavenly face, a drop of hot grease fell from the candle onto his shoulder. This, of course, was very awakening, and he opened his eyes and took a square look at her without saying a word. Then in the batting of an eye he spread his white wings and flitted out of the window. She knew in a moment that her youthful husband was none other than Cupid; and as he went through the window she took after him, and yelled at the top of her voice for him to wait a minute as she wanted to explain things; but he just kept on flying. In trying to follow him she fell out of the window and hit the ground very hard. As she lay there in the dust, almost exhausted, she heard Cupid's voice:

"I took you in out of the wet against my immortal mother's wishes," he said. "Like all women, you are curious and shy on confidence. You have taken me for a snake and wanted to cut my head off. Oh, but you are a good one. I will tell you, my little girl, that love and suspicion will not mix; so you had better go home to your sisters and get some more advice from them, you may need it in your business. I am through with you; I say I am through; so good-by, Psyche, good-by," and away he flew through the air up among the stars.

Psyche had nothing left except a good supply of lamentations. When she came to herself she looked around and, to her great surprise, the garden and palace had been removed. After figuring awhile to get her bearings, she found that she was in a woods pasture, near the village in which she had lived. She went to the house, told her people how it happened and how badly she felt over it. The sisters played they were almost killed with grief, although they were laughing in their sleeves. They rejoiced that their scheme to separate Cupid and Psyche had worked well.

The next morning the sisters climbed the mountain bright and early to see Zephyr about a trip to Cupid's home. They were desirous that the prince of love might select one of them in place of Psyche. When they reached the mountain top one called to Zephyr to give her a boost into the air, never imagining that he would refuse. She made a jump and went about twenty-one feet into space. Zephyr failed to support her, and she fell about 18,000 feet to the bottom of a canyon. Her remains were taken home soaked in embalming fluid.

Psyche wandered around at all hours, worrying about her marriage failure, and refusing to take any food except a griddle cake now and then. One day she looked up at the top of a high mountain and discovered a fine temple. She thought perhaps Cupid might live there, and if he did, there might be a chance to see him and square herself. When she arrived the temple proved to be a corn crib. In it was a great lot of oats, corn, millet seed, fodder, broomcorn, timothy hay and seed wheat, besides a number of farming implements. She made herself busy putting everything in order. While thus engaged the holy Ceres, the owner of the crib, came in.

Psyche told her the story of her past life. Ceres was sorry for her, and gave her a lot of good advice on how to get Cupid back again.

"Go direct to Venus, your mother-in-law," she said, "and lay your case before her. Tell her you are willing to do any old kind of hard work just to prove to her that in the future you will cut out all your curiosity, and that when Cupid tells you a thing you will believe him, because he is your lord and master. Now, to show Venus that you are willing to act properly, tell her you will put out Monday's washing, do all the baking for Sunday, and will even go out and plant the garden stuff if she so desires. Of course, it is hardly probable that she will

SHE FELL ABOUT 18,000 FEET TO THE BOTTOM OF A CANYON.

310

ask you to shovel coal, saw wood or dig wells, but if she does, why, tackle it anyway, and perhaps by your being good she may forgive you and fix it with Cupid so you can join hands again and forever be happy."

So Psyche hied herself away to the temple of Venus. On the way she had many thoughts of how she would brace the angry goddess. She did not know but that Venus would throw her out bodily, but she was dead anxious to take the chance. When she arrived at the temple Venus gave her a look that was nothing short of a downright freeze-out. Talk about a woman's scorn; Venus sure enough had her scorning gown on that day, and the way she talked to Psyche was something fierce.

When she had tired herself out talking she concluded her roasting by telling Psyche that she might win Cupid back if she would undergo a lot of hardships and perform a number of impossible feats. Psyche told her that she would undertake any kind of labor that might be required of her; then Venus ordered her to be led out to the barn, where there were several hundred bushels of pigeon feed, such as flaxseed, corn, black eyed peas, barley, clover seed, hemp seed, navy beans, castor beans and wild turnip seed, all mixed up in one great big heap. She was commanded to pick these seeds over and put each kind in a separate pile by 6 o'clock in the evening. This was a test of Psyche's housewifery. When the little girl looked at that inextricable heap she turned pale. She sat down on a feed-box and heaved a sigh which Cupid heard across a two-acre field. He knew what was up, and he lost no time in stirring up about eighty bushels of field ants to help her out. The ants worked diligently, and the job was completed before 6 o'clock. When the last seed was in its place, every ant disappeared. A little later Venus returned having spent all the afternoon at a goddess'

"TAKE THE ROAD THAT WILL LEAD YOU BY CERBERUS—THE BIG ROAN DOG WITH THREE HEADS.

reunion. When she saw that the work was completed, she said to Psyche:

"Now, you can't fool me; this is a put up job, as I know you have been assisted in some secret way. No doubt my son Cupid has had his fingers in this work, so you will not be allowed one bit of credit for your labor."

She then threw her a chunk of stale rye bread and left Psyche to sleep in the haymow alone.

Next morning Venus went out to the barn and ordered Psyche to a certain grove by the river, where she would find a flock of sheep with golden fleece, from the back of each of which she must bring a sample of wool. When she reached the river bank she heard the river god say:

"Be careful about pulling wool, because the sheep will not stand for it. They are under the influence of the rising sun and blind with rage and the wool is too hot to pull. Some of those big rams are also likely to butt you, and if they do you will land in the middle of the river. The way to get wool is to wait until noon, as the sheep go into the woods to rest at that time, rub up against the trunks of trees as they pass along and leave bunches of wool sticking to the bark. When they go away you can get all the wool you can carry." She took his advice, and at noontide she pulled an armful of golden wool and took it to Venus, as requested. Venus told her she knew full well some god had assisted her, as she deemed it impossible she should have plucked the wool so quickly from such a dangerous bunch of all-wool merinos.

"I will put you to another test," she said, "and this time I will keep you guessing, as it will be a severe one. I will yet find out to my entire satisfaction whether a cheap mortal like you is worthy of my son. Take this chocolate-cream box and make your way to the infernal shades. Hand it to Proserpine to fill with some of her

"YOU MUST SEE CHARON, WHO RUNS THE FERRY ACROSS THAT INKY-LOOKING RIVER."

beauty paint. Do not forget to tell her it is for me. .You must return before evening, as I have a date to-night with the gods and goddesses, and I need the contents of the beauty box with which to retouch my face. Tell her, also, that I have been sitting up day and night doctoring Cupid's burned shoulder upon which you dropped hot grease, and with the loss of sleep I have lost some of my beauty; in fact, I look like the deuce."

Psyche dreaded the trip, as she had never traveled the road to the dark shades below, and besides she had not the least idea of how to start. She climbed to the crag of a mountain to give herself a good send-off. She thought the best way to make a short trip would be to jump head first into space. As she was about to make the fatal leap she heard a voice, which said:

"Say, Psyche, what is the matter with you? Are you going to commit suicide? Don't you know if you make that leap you will break your marriage vow? Now, don't be foolish., If you are on a trip to Pluto's realm, take the road that will lead you by Cerberus—the big roan dog with three heads. That is the only safe route. You must see Charon, who runs the ferry across that inky-looking river, and make arrangements to have him set you over. Fix it with him so you can get back, for if you fail to return—well, you know the rest. When you see Proserpine, get your box of beauty paint and start back at once, for that is a bad place in which to loaf. Above all things, don't get a curious spell on you and try to open the box—remember that."

She made the trip in safety; got the box filled with the precious commodity, and started to return to the temple of Venus. On the road she was seized with a curiosity to open that box and put a little of the beauty paint on her own face, in order to look well in the sight of Cupid. She opened the box—and found it empty. That

HE THEN SENT MERCURY TO BRING PSYCHE UP TO THE HEAVENLY ASSEMBLY.

moment she dropped to the ground, took on one of those deep, Stygian sleeps, and appeared as one dead.

By this time Cupid had about recovered from his burn and was able to fly about. He was tired being alone, and the moment Psyche fell in the road he had a presentiment that something was wrong. He crawled out through the window of his mother's temple and flew to where Psyche was sleeping. He took the spell from her, put the beauty paint in the box and reproved her for being so curious. He loved her, and wanted to break her of the curiosity habit. He pointed up toward the earth and told her to hasten to his mother with the box, and not to worry any longer as he would do the rest.

While she was on the road, Cupid went over to see Jupiter, and laid his case before him, as he was very anxious to get Psyche back again and make her immortal. Jupiter was kind to Cupid, and to show that he was all right he took a trip to the temple of Venus. He gave Venus a nice long hot-air talk and got her consent to allow the pair of lovers to get together again. He then sent Mercury to bring Psyche up to the heavenly assembly. When she arrived, they had a big time in her honor. She took a drink with a few of the way-up gods and was made immortal. She also got the assurance from them that Cupid would never again give her the shake.

Here endeth the story of Cupid and Psyche.

A PROFESSIONAL WEEPER.

SAM W. HURDLE was born, by permission, a little after sunset in the fall of 1859, and has lived continuously since. At the age of two he asked his father if he was living in a free country. His father replied that the country was tamped full of freedom clean up to its throatlatch; but that, unfortunately, he was born in the District of Columbia, and would never be allowed to vote in that community, unless it was on the quiet, and even then his vote would not be counted. From that hour Sam commenced to weep, and he has continued weeping unto this day.

He has a technical training in several professions; but weeping is his specialty. He will go three or four miles out of his way just to find something to weep about. The habit is so fastened upon his system that he seems to enjoy it.

In his youth he became a first-class somnambulist. Even yet he will somnamble into a graveyard when the night is wild and dangerous. It is on such occasions he turns on the spigot and the briny fluid flows. He will lean up against the silent tombs and sob and sigh over all denominations. The fact that it might be a strange graveyard would make no difference.

The day he was twenty-one he said to his father:

"Pa, I am of age to-day, and I desire to do for myself."

"What business have you decided to take up?" asked his father.

"I think I would like to be a traveling man."

"A traveling man?"

"Yes, sir. I know I would be a great success."

"But, my son, that business is liable to get you into bad habits, as you would have so many chances to learn how to drink rum and play seven-up."

"No, pa, never! Not on your zinc etching. There is only one line of goods I would sell, and there would be no occasion for me to use emery paper on my breath at any time, as no one ever calls for drinks while in that business."

"What line of goods do you refer to?"

"Gravestones."

"Well, I guess you are right. Selling gravestones is about the most serious business you could choose, so you have my full consent."

Sam was not long in securing a position with a gravestone concern. They gave him a long list of people's names from whom he might be able to take some orders. He told them that he did not care for the list, as he would pick out his own customers. "I have a system of my own," he said. "The only persons I will call upon are those who have just lost a relative."

His idea was a good one, as he made it a point to go right into a house where the family was grieving. He would sympathize with them for a few minutes, and then begin to weep. He was considered the best all-round single-handed weeper in the country. It was then he would tell his business, and between sobs he would make a cut price on a tall gravestone. Being such a successful weeper, he always touched the hearts of the family, and took an order.

While in this business, he wept so long and faithfully that his lachrymal ducts got clogged up. When I say lachrymal, I do not know what I am talking about, since that word belongs to a dialect spoken only by physicians. I will simply say tear duct and let it go at that. Any way when Sam's tear ducts refused to work it assisted him materially in weeping, for then he cried all the time. He did not wait for weeping hours, but just kept on crying day and night. If any one stopped to tell him a joke or a funny story, tears would stream down his cheeks, as though he had lost all his relatives.

His business kept on increasing. There was not a graveyard in the whole country where his brand of hand polished monuments could not be seen.

While he was very well pleased with the business, he fancied he would like to try something else and obtained employment with an accident insurance company. At this he was also very successful, as he made it a point to talk to the wives of men who were employed at some hazardous work.

The following will give some idea of how he put his case before a woman whose husband was liable to come home any night packed in saw-dust:

"My dear madam (turning on his tears), excuse me for being a rank stranger to you; but my name is Sam Hurdle. I am representing the Death Guarantee Accident Insurance Company (sobs and weeps), and I came here to bring you a gleam of hope. Is your husband insured against accidents and death?"

"No, sir, he is not; but I have often thought he ought to be."

"Well, I am very sorry for you, madam. (Then his leaky tear ducts would shower tears on the floor like drops of rain on a tin roof.) You see, my object is to insure your husband against getting killed. It is of grave importance to you, madam. You know not the hour when your husband may be run over by a train of sixteen heavy freight cars, and be brought to your very door a mass of unrecognizable humanity. Think of it, madam; (voice trembling) you would be left destitute, homeless, hungry, helpless and a poor widow woman with nine children. Can you contemplate, my dear woman, what an awful thing it is to be left without a husband, without a cent, and bareheaded. You may not have even a bacon rind with which to grease the skillet. So I say, woman, do not procrastinate, but have your husband insure in our company at once."

The poor woman was moved to tears herself. She requested Sam to say nothing more on the subject; as she was willing to get her husband insured for five thousand dollars. She requested him to call the next day, as by that time she would have sold most of her furniture and could pay the premium.

When Sam thought he was the least bit shy on weeping power, he would go into the woods and sit on a barbed wire fence for a spell, as he knew this would increase his grief. In the insurance business he did well; but again he decided to try something else. This time he went to New York city. The first thing he did was to look up a morgue, to keep his tear valves in good working order until he found the kind of work that suited him. After weeping in the morgue for several days, he heard through an undertaker of a vacancy in the position of official pall-bearer. It did not take Sam long to secure the job. He gave references which showed him to be one of the most dead-in-earnest mourners in the whole country.

One of the three other pall-bearers with whom he worked daily said to him one day as the four were returning from the cemetery:

"Mr. Hurdle, I would like to ask you a question. I have made twenty-seven trips to the cemetery with you, and notice that each time you were very much aggrieved and wept bitterly. Now, may I ask, if all these corpses were related to you while they lived?"

"No, not one of them; they were all dead strangers to me."

"Yes, I knew that they were all dead, but never for once did I think they were strangers, the way you took on."

"The reason I wept, is because that is my business. I have a standing challenge to outweep any man that ever attended a funeral. Weeping is in my line. I weep all the time, I weep for and against, and I weep on all occasions. One day I saw a woodman in the forest with his ax, and I wept. I wept the night I got married, and I have wept ever since."

He acted as official pall-bearer for several years, and it has been said since he left New York that he was the best catch-as-catch-can weeper that America has ever produced.

After giving up the pall-bearing business he drifted to Chicago, where he took up the business of singing at funerals. At this work he has no peer. He only sings now as a kind of a side line. He is principally engaged in conducting a haberdashery in the Fisher building. In conversation some time ago, I asked him what class of songs he sang at funerals.

"I sometimes sing 'Beyond the Smiling and the Weeping,' " he said.

"Speaking of weeping, do you weep any harder when **you** sing that song, than you do in any other?"

"No, I can't say that I do. You see, a professional weeper weeps about the same way all the time. Once in a while I sing 'Art thou weary, art thou languid.' This song is a favorite of mine, as it is so applicable to my profession. By the way, have you ever seen me languid or weary?"

"No, I cannot say that I have."

"Well, sir, you should see me get on one of my loose-fitting languid spells. I never do anything by halves. When I get languid I am truly serious about it."

"How is it that you went into the furnishing goods business. Is that considered a serious proposition?"

"Is it? Well, you should try it once in Chicago. No man living could make it pay unless he was serious clean up to the neck. That is the only way I can win out. I do not have to weep in this business, but, sir, it stands me in hand to keep by me a car load of conversational power and a devil of a lot of seriousness. Besides this business, every once in a while I get a chance to sell a gravestone, and that helps some."

"With all the success you have had in your several branches of business, you have been able to save up quite a little of this world's goods, have you not?"

"Well, now, I do not know that it is any of your business; however, I have made in my time a great deal of money. It was not properly cured, however, or else it was frost bitten or sunburnt, or something of that kind. Anyway it would not keep."

"Excuse me for interrupting, but you say you still sell gravestones?"

"Yes, now and then when I get a chance; but I cannot sell one unless I prepare for it."

"Prepare for it? What do you mean; get yourself in talking order?"

"No, I have to get myself in weeping order."

"I thought you told me you were always in weeping order."

"So I did, but I forgot to tell you that since I have been in the furnishing goods line my physician has introduced two silver nails into my tear ducts. These cut out the weeping and the extra sobs when I do not need them. So you see when I get a chance to sell a gravestone I just pull out these two six-penny silver nails and start the tears flowing. Oh, yes, sir, I do certainly know my business. I met a woman the other day—a girl of rare old vintage. She had lost her sweetheart in Cuba and she wanted a monument to place at the head of his grave. Well, I lifted the silver nails and cried her into the notion of buying a thousand-dollar gravestone. I'll tell you, Mr. Woodruf, the right kind of weeping pays, and if you ever need any of my weeps, send for me. The only thing I hate about the business is this: I am, of course, cognizant of the fact—that awful, inevitable fact—that the time will come when I must lie down and turn my corn-laden toes to the cerulean skies, and I am afraid the friends who come to weep over my dead body will turn the weeping into a joke and make a farce of my funeral."

HE SAVED MY LIFE.

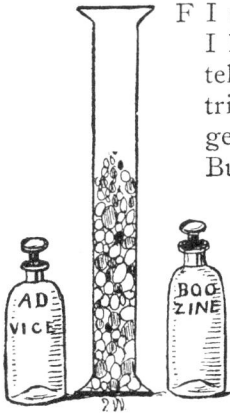

F I should live to be 87 years old (which I know I will, if Father Time does not telephone me to make an unexpected trip to the unknown), I can never forget the wise counsel of Dr. George F. Butler, vice president and medical superintendent of the Alma, Mich., Sanitarium.

He is a man of hiuraligy and strong psychobunction. It matters not with what a patient is pestered, whether lightness of the top flat, insomnia of the liver, hemorrhage of the roechinaeus or complete disenintegration of the adipose tissue; he can make them look new and put them on a healthy basis, so they can go out into the cold world and shift for themselves. It is not my intention to go too deep into the science of medicine or the effects and results of diseases in man, as I am better posted on the treatment of ailing horses and mules, having been a student for some time in a veterinary college.

It always hurts me, when I wish to run in a lot of heavy weight panegyrics to fit some one to whom I wish to show my gratitude and full grown appreciations for services rendered. I only wish I was away up in high C on the doctor business, then I could put a dress suit on my language and show Dr. Butler how I feel toward him for saving my life without the aid of drugs.

Two years ago, I was under the impression that my time on this earth was short, as I verily believed that I was the proprietor of an incurable disease. I could see myself slowly drifting into my last resting place. I well knew that I could not live long, as I had every reason to believe I was afflicted with that dreaded disease—locomotor ataxia. I called at the doctor's office and made a clean breast of my trouble.

"What reason have you to believe that you have locomotor ataxia?" he inquired.

"I have every reason to think so. My nerves show signs of degeneration. This alone is discouraging, as I have always prided myself on my nerve. I have ocular symptoms; that is, seeing things double. Then my inability to get a sudden move on myself is very noticeable. To maintain my equilibrium is a difficult task. My feet will not track. My walk is on the serpentine order. There are times when it is necessary to have a man on each side of me. Then my speech is not reliable, as I have an impediment."

"Are these symptoms continuous?"

"Oh, no, doctor. I have them just once in awhile."

"Well, I am afraid as a diagnostician you are not up to date. Can you walk straight in the dark?"

"Not at all times. I sometimes walk a little on the bias in day light."

"You see, locomotor ataxia—often called tabes dorsalis, progressive spinal paralysis, neuro-spinal tabes, or progressive locomotor asynergia—is a very serious trouble."

"Now, doctor, if you have any respect for me, stop right there. Don't throw those big words around so careless like, unless you can in some way cheapen them

I CALLED AT THE DOCTOR'S OFFICE AND MADE A CLEAN BREAST OF MY TROUBLES.

327

and cut them down to my size. When it comes to speaking the Choctaw and Sioux languages, why, I am right there with the goods; but beyond that I am a dead one. If you want to talk to me about this disease, please make it a point to use words with not more than two joints in them."

"Why, these are very cheap words. Take, for instance tabes dorsalis; the Hippocratic authors several hundred years before the birth of Christ considered that a very common word; and a word so gray with age should not appear to you as a stranger. Locomotor ataxia is a degenerative disease, having a front seat in the sensory nervous system; affecting, as a rule, both cerebral and peripheral portions. In cases fully developed a patient may be on the look out for radiating, defective tactile pains; loss of muscle reflex action, more especially the patella tendon reflex. You see, when the nervous system is affected it is characterized clinically by incoördination, trophic and sensory disturbances. I use these common terms to make it clear to your mind. Are you troubled with biliousness?"

"No, sir, none to speak of, only a phrenologist once told me I had a bilious temperament, while my brother had a sanguine temperament. I thought at the time he would not have said this about my brother if he had not been red headed."

"Run your tongue out about eighteen inches, please."

As I did so he turned my face to one side.

"How long have you been carrying this vulcanized breath around with you?" he asked.

"I really cannot say," I replied; "my friends notice it more than I do."

"I will prescribe some disinfectant, for if a weakly person should get one whiff it would more than likely produce blind staggers, which might prove fatal. I notice that you do not need pants and vest, the coat on your tongue is heavy enough to take the place of a whole suit. Are you troubled any with rheumatism or quinsy?"

"Not to my knowledge."

"You say that you have double visions."

"Yes, sir, once in a while."

"When are you troubled that way?"

"Only when I go out with the gang and take in a few hundred places where liquor is sold."

"Does the gang see double?"

"Oh, yes, sir; they all get into the same fix. The fact is, they have the same symptoms."

"Does your hair pull much?"

"Very much."

"Have you headache?"

"I should say so."

"Do you have a bad taste in your mouth the next day?"

"Do I? Well, I should remark; the worst ever. It is simply fierce."

"Is it on the occasion of going out with the gang, as you call it that you do not walk straight?"

"Yes, sir; it is on such occasions that I have all the symptoms of locomotor ataxia."

"Oh, yes, I see. Well, you have, as I thought, made a wrong diagnosis of your case. It is not locomotor ataxia that you have. It is what we call acute rum-ingitis. All you have to do is to take an oath that you will stop drinking. No doubt you can proudly boast of being the hero of many jags, and it is time for you to stop: then all those disagreeable symptoms will leave you. Your system is not constructed to stand up under so much poison. A man's being is like the workings of a watch. If you treat a watch well it will run for you and keep time; but if you open it up to disagreeable elements the hair spring

will rust and you couldn't hire it to run without treat‚
ment.   Every little wheel and spring has a duty which
it will not perform unless properly cared for and treated
right.   The same with your system; every organ has a
function which it cannot perform unless you treat it well.
If you have a sick liver, your whole system is on the bum
until you treat your liver as it should be treated.   You
cannot blame a liver for going to sleep on you, and not
doing its turn when you give it wormwood in place of
balm.   An actor will not half work if he knows his salary
is not coming on time.   So there you are; now will you
be good?

"Liquor is a terrible thing to fool with my friend.   It
is the disgrace of a nation, the contaminater of politics
and the disturber of society.   Many people try to handle
liquor in moderation, but they soon grow tired of that,
and then they begin to handle it in gallon jugs.   When
you want a drink go to a pump, then the board of health
will not be after you about the condition of your breath."

"Your advice is good, doctor, but while I think of it
(pardon me for changing the subject), is there any cure
for locomotor ataxia?"

"Yes, there is a cure.   The only thing a patient can
do is to take a trip abroad in a sailing vessel, one that is
leaky and unsafe.   The trip should be taken during the
equinoxial storms and be sure to board a ship that can
never weather the storm.   That is a sure cure."

"I thank you very much, doctor, for this consultation.
I will begin at once to change my ways."

From that day to this I have never allowed whisky,
beer, gin, wine, porter or ale to pass my lips.   I stick
right to brandy

A SUCCESSFUL FAILURE.

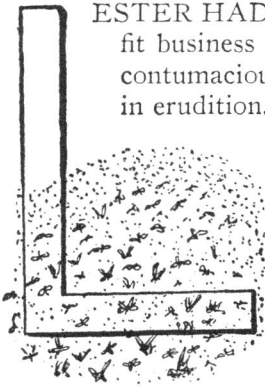

ESTER HADLEY admitted openly that as a misfit business man he was a failure. Yet he was contumacious and much stronger in satire than in erudition. For a silly reason his father took him out of school at an early age. He had gone through subtraction and multiplication, but his father stopped him, for the reason he did not believe in division. He said he had toiled for many years to save up some thing for old age, and he meant to keep it. He thought division was a poor thing to teach a boy. So Lester had to leave school. This, of course, put a damper on his success in life. He was ambitious, however, and wanted to make his mark.

At times he was kept busy setting down the innumerable drove of thoughts that trotted through the broad thoroughfare of his brain. He considered each thought as it passed. One was a bulldog in war; another, a lamb in peace, and another, a belligerent, which he might or might not stop to placate. His object was to buckle on to a happy thought; one that he could harness up and hitch to the jump-cart of prosperity and drive away to success.

One day he was firmly impressed with the idea that he should launch into the horseshoeing business. The next day, he would call himself an idiot for having such a crazy thought, as he knew that he was cut out for a soldier. And so on, he kept himself busy guessing.

In his early life he was told by his father that he should be an artist. This he tried for three years, but somehow he failed. The best he could do was to draw his salary. He went back to his father with a depleted exchequer and a full set of custom-made vituperations. His father did not take kindly to this style of art, so in an angry moment he told the boy that he could consider his propinquity called off.

He then went out into the woods, where he could be alone, and had another reverie of thought chasing. His irregular train of thoughts got uncoupled and went into the ditch. When he recovered he was forced to believe by his own influence and recommendation that he was a natural born poet. He went at this work with all seriousness and earnestness and kept himself busy for many months. He is today the author of several hundred poems. He submitted many of them to papers and magazines, but it was at a time when they were all overstocked. He waited long in vain to see one of his poems in print. His physician told him he had a wrong impression about his ability, and that he was not a poet, but was afflicted with St. Vitus' dance.

The question before him then was what to try next. Some one told him money was to be made with insect powder, so he started a factory.

The first thing he did after he was ready to supply the demand was to get out a card reading:

"Get ready to fight. The time is upon us for bugs.

"Do flies make too free with you?

"Are the fangs of a bed bug poisonous to you?

"Does your husband leave the screen door open?

"Do cockroaches roost in your kitchen?

"Are the women folks bothered with fleas?

"Do gnats use your milk pan as a swimming pool?

"Does it bother you for a couple of thousand flies to walk out of a pan of molasses and light on your face?

"If this is the case at your house, then call for Lester Hadley's Sudden Death Insect Powder. I guarantee that if a living insect ever takes one snootful of this powder it will get on its back and play dead, and the part it plays will be no josh. Get your insects in line and begin hostilities at once.

"Cash price, 25 cents—credit, $9."

The card was a hit, and his business was good from the start. He was happy to think that he had lassoed a thought that would win.

Every one who used his powder swore flat footed it was the best knock-down-and-drag-out exterminator that ever shut off the wind of an insect. He received several testimonials on its merits. One read:

"Dear Sir: After seeing your advertisement, I tried your powder. I may say beforehand that our neighbors accused us of having more fleas than any one in the county. I bought one package of your powder on a credit basis. I got a gallon or so of insects together and began to feed them—not with a spoon, but with dexterity. Fleas are phlebotomists by profession, and we have been flea-bitten and flea-ridden until we were about ready to flee from home. We are truly thankful to get a powder that will make an insect behave.

"Yours truly,   A SUFFERER."

Another wrote:

"Dear Mr. Hadley: This is to say that I tried your Sudden Death Insect Powder, and am frank to confess that it is just the thing to rid the place of the regular summer household pests. Any brand of insects that dallies with your powder is a dead one. I have recommended it to several of my friends, as I know they need it.

"Yours very respt.,   SILAS DOONE."

All this made Lester feel that his fortune was made, and on the strength of such good prospects he decided to get married, as he had saved up a few dollars for that purpose. The one of his choice was a little, black-eyed beauty, who could sing like a meadow-lark. She could smoke a violet-scented, gold-tipped cigarette, and handle a carbine like a sportsman. Her saucy, brunette face and big graphite eyes kept Lester in a whirl of admiration, and made him a most passionate adorer. He was aware of the fact that she had other adorers—more than she could count on her fingers. She would lend a friendly ear to their protestations, but that was all. She cared not for them.

Lester was her homestead and pre-emption claim all sowed and planted, and she expected to harvest a crop of joy and bliss. If there was anything delusive and shadowy about this brilliant, sparkling stream of love, Lester did not know it.

The wedding was to take place at night.

While Lester was somewhat pastoral in his manners, his finance was a metropolitan pure and simple. The wedding came off as per arrangement and both seemed happy. They started in light housekeeping and the business continued good until winter. The first cold snap came early and froze all the insects. And to make matters worse, one night his factory burned to the ground. He had no insurance, and consequently all he had left was a gasoline cook stove and a town-raised wife. Everything went wrong. His money was gone, his business was wrecked. His little bewildering queen stood for this some time without complaining, but at last grew dissatisfied. Her hopes pickled and her love curdled. Her golden noontide did not loom up much brighter than a magic lantern. The poor woman's thoughts drifted backward. The joy of her life at home in the whirl of gay society came back to her like a high ball to a thirsty printer on a country daily.

She was sick at heart and could think only of her home. Her husband was up a sapling and her love for him was on the wane. He had admitted to her before marriage that as a business man he was a successful failure, but the pupils of her eyes were dilated and she could not see very well. What a sad thing it is when love is so blind that lovers cannot get permission from society to wear green goggles.

It is true Lester loved her with a passion simply savage—fierce—one of those burning loves—but he well knew that he could not hold on to her unless he provided. It was the same old story, "When poverty comes in at the kitchen door, love makes a sneak through the transom."

One afternoon Mrs. Hadley visited an old schoolmate who had just arrived from her home town. She was stopping at one of the leading hotels and was registered as Mrs. Lorena Baxter, which was perfectly correct.

They were more than delighted to meet and their ecstasies lasted about twenty minutes.

"Pray tell me all about yourself, Nettie," Mrs. Baxter said (she had always called Mrs. Hadley Nettie), "and tell me all the news; don't leave out anything."

"Well, I'll tell you, Lorena; it's a sad story."

"Why, does he drink?"

"No, no, not that. He is shy on funds, and you know me. No man can trifle with my affections unless he has a large amount of lucre.   To make a long story short, Lester is short on lucre, and there you are, and here am I —all broken up like flint stones from a rock crusher.   I have not been out for a 'time' since I became his wife."

"Oh, isn't that a shame!" said Lorena.   "Wait a minute, there must be a button around my room somewhere. Yes, here it is; I'll just push it."   She walked up to the left of the dresser and rang the bell.   A waiter was soon on the spot to answer the call.

"Dearest, what will you have?" Lorena asked.

"Oh, I don't know exactly; what are you going to take?"

"Now, never mind me, Nettie; take what you want."

"Well, how would a gin fizz go?"

"It will go with me all right."

"Very well, let it go double."

"That suits me to a tyt.   Waiter, two large gin fizzes, please.   Tell the man they are for adults."

"You know, Lorena, Lester despises to see a woman drink; but never mind, I'm going to drink any way, and if he does not like it he can lump it.   For all that, I am going to be careful what I drink.   As long as I live I never want to see another whisky punch.   Just before I left home to come here and marry this 30-cent husband of mine I went out one evening with Laura Gilson, and we had about forty of those nasty punches.   And sick! Oh my, oh me!   I was the sickest girl you ever met. Well, no wonder we were both paralyzed."   Just then there was a knock at the door.

"Come," Lorena commanded.   It was the waiter with the fizzes, which were soon hidden away.   Then followed a long talk of old times.   Lorena felt a thirst coming on and the waiter was called again.

"Two more fizzes, please."

Then there was some more talk and another pair of fizzes. So the afternoon was spent in joy and laughter. Nettie went home in a carriage. When she met her husband she swore there were nine of them.

Lester almost fainted. He stood in the middle of the room transfixed. When his wife returned to a speaking condition she told him how it happened, and assured him she had taken but one drink, that was all. He now regrets all the endearing words and impassioned caresses that he had wasted on her. He had worshiped her madly, but now it was all off. He flew into a paroxysm of rage and told her to go out and throw mud at herself, as he was through with her and was going to step down and out.

He very soon made arrangements to send her back to her people, as his love for her had soured, and he wanted to be alone.

Now that his insect powder factory was in ashes, and his wife was not what she seemed, he was further up the sapling than ever; and besides he was a confirmed misogamist.

He remembered that in days past he had read up considerably on phrenology and a thought struck him that he might go on the road and do well examining heads; as that would only require sufficient capital to get to the first town. He walked thirty-four miles to a village in the country and advertised himself in the following manner:

"To-night! To-night!

"Prof. Lester Hadley.

"The wonder of the age.

"The most marvelous phrenologist in modern times. He will examine your head and tell you what you are.

"Come early and get good seats.

"Admission, free."

On account of the admission being free, he had a full house. He expected to make his money by giving charts. He began in the old way by getting a committee of four or five to walk up on the stage and blindfold him; then bring up some one from the audience and he would tell who and what he was. An old, respectable residenter was persuaded to go up and make the test.

"Ladies and gentlemen," said the renowned phrenologist, "this head is a wonder. It has more combinations of real devilment in it than any head I have ever examined. This man is a horse thief and a traitor."

Just then the residenter got up from his seat and demanded that the committee take the blind off the professor. For a few minutes there was a rough stage. No tragedy had ever been played there to equal it. When the residenter finished his work the professor looked as though he was ready to be embalmed. He was taken to his hotel on a stretcher. It was some weeks before he could walk without crutches.

When he was able to recognize his own face in a mirror he began to look about for a business where there was not so much risk.

One of his uncles was a minister of the gospel, and was considered a good preacher. Lester thought that he might do worse than go to preaching. He had put in much time on theology, and he thought perhaps that might be his calling. He had in one way and another been called down on everything else he ever tried and he was now ready to try some other business.

He said to me one morning:

"Don't you know, I think I will take up the ministry. What do you think about it?"

FOR A FEW MINUTES THERE WAS A ROUGH STAGE.

"I do not exactly know, Lester, but I rather think you
would make a rattling good preacher; besides, there is a
great field for that work. What denomination do you
lean toward?"

"I am an old-fashioned Methodist, South."

"Is there much difference in the Methodist, South and
the Methodist, North?"

"No, not much. You see the Methodists, North take
in members on six months' probation, while the Methodists, South take them in right on the jump."

"You will find one great drawback preaching that doctrine in your case."

"Why so?"

"On account of your father taking you out of school
so young and not allowing you to study division. The
conference will perhaps send you to a field of action
where the members are not used to fine sermons. Somewhere in a backwoods district, where you will be known
as a circuit rider. In such cases you will find stewards of
the church whose business it is to go around the country
and see all the members and collect supplies for the
preacher. When I say supplies, I mean farm produce,
butter, eggs, cheese, bacon, lard, cordwood, soap, apple-
butter, molasses, young shoats, chickens and such like.
Now, this all comes under the head of division. You
should be able at the close of each Sunday sermon, before
the hat is passed, to disertate at length on long division,
and show fully the efficacy of it. In other words, teach
your members how to divide. I can see, however, you
are bound to preach, and all I can say is, I wish you good
luck."

It came to pass that he did preach. But he changed his
religion three times. He started in as a Methodist, South,

changed to a Presbyterian and wound up as a Hard-Shell Baptist.   His followers became dissatisfied with him, got cold feet and refused to support him.   The last I heard of him he was braking on a freight train out in Montana.